T. S. Eliot

A Chronology of his Life and Works

T. S. ELIOT
A Chronology of his Life and Works

CAROLINE BEHR

ST. MARTIN'S PRESS
NEW YORK

First published in the United States of America in 1983

Library of Congress Cataloging in Publication Data

Behr, Caroline.
    T. S. Eliot, a chronology of his life and works.

    1. Eliot, T. S. (Thomas Stearnes), 1888—1965—Chronology.
2. Poets, American—20th century—Biography. I. Title. II. Title:
TS Eliot, a chronology of his life and works.
PS3509.L43Z642 1983   821'.912   82-16716
ISBN 0-312-82185-9

Typeset by
STYLESET LIMITED
Salisbury, Wiltshire

Printed in Hong Kong

Contents

Preface   vii

Text   1

Works List   89

Bibliography   121

Acknowledgements   123

Preface

In order to chart the main lines of Eliot's thought and work, I have, of necessity, had to select those items from Eliot's vast output which seemed to me most important; but readers will find a comprehensive Works List, chronologically arranged, on page 89. Eliot's essays, articles and reviews are mentioned as they first appear; subsequent publication in book form can also be found in the Works List. This information could not have been collected without Donald Gallup's *Bibliography* of Eliot, justly described by Bernard Bergonzi as 'magnificent'.

With the lack of any authenticated biography of Eliot, I have tried to cover most of the biographical material that has been published, and readers will find a list of source books in the Bibliography on page 121. The number of published letters by Eliot is so scarce that I have inserted the source after each one mentioned, for example (Valerie Eliot, 1971), which will allow the reader easily to trace the actual text for himself.

The eventual publication of more of Eliot's letters, and the eventual release of material from various libraries, as well as memoirs still to be written, should continue to throw light upon the life and thought of this most distinguished poet and thinker.

Preface

1888

→ **26 September:** Thomas Stearns Eliot is born in St Louis, Missouri, the youngest of a family of six (four girls and two boys). His grandfather, William Greenleaf Eliot, came from a long-established New England family descended from Andrew Eliot, who emigrated from East Coker, Somerset, in 1669. William Greenleaf Eliot settled in St Louis in 1831, hoping, as a young Protestant pastor, to found a Unitarian mission there. During the Civil War he and his wife organized a service for the wounded; in 1856 he established a mission Free School; in 1857 he founded Washington University in St Louis, and later its preparatory school, Smith Academy, and a girls' school, the Mary Institute. In 1872 he became president of Washington University. His second son, Henry Ware Eliot, born in 1843, was T. S. Eliot's father. In 1869 Henry Ware Eliot married Charlotte Champe Eliot, also from an old Massachusetts family, and later to write a life of her distinguished father-in-law and a dramatic poem on the life of Savanarola. Henry Ware Eliot was first secretary, then chairman and later president of a brick-making firm, the Hydraulic Brick Company.

1889-1897

→ Eliot spends his early years living with his family in St Louis. In 1930, in a letter to *The St Louis Post-Dispatch*, Eliot will recall his childhood in St Louis; and will describe in 1953, in *American Literature and American Language*, how he was brought up to respect the 'Law of Public Service' operating in the three areas of religion, the community and education. The Eliot family spend summers at Henry Ware Eliot's house near East Gloucester in Massachusetts; in 1928, in his preface to Edgar Mowrer's *This American World*, Eliot will describe how he became aware of the difference in the landscapes of St Louis and New England; and in 1932, in the series of lectures to become *The Use of Poetry and the Use of Criticism* (1933), he will describe the influence of the New England landscape on his poetry.

1898

→ Eliot is sent to Smith Academy, St Louis, founded by his grandfather; where he stays until 1905. In 1932, in the series of lectures to become

The Use of Poetry and the Use of Criticism (1933) Eliot will describe his interests in poetry while at Smith Academy.

1905

February/June: Eliot's earliest printed works appear in the school magazine, the *Smith Academy Record*: a humourous doggerel poem, 'A Fable for Feasters' (February 1905); two schoolboy stories, 'A Tale of a Whale' and 'The Man Who Was King' (April and June 1905), reflecting Eliot's boyhood fondness for adventure and sea stories; and 'A Lyric' ('If Time and Space, as Sages say') (April 1905).

Autumn: Eliot is sent for a year to Milton Academy, a select preparatory school in New England, where he concentrates on history, Latin and physics.

1906

October: Eliot starts his first term at Harvard University. Conrad Aiken, a fellow student, later to become a poet and lifelong friend, remembers Eliot as 'a singularly attractive, tall and rather dapper young man, with a somewhat Lamian smile'. Aiken describes Harvard itself as: 'little more than a village . . . Lilacs and white picket fences under elms, horse-drawn watering-carts to lay the dust in the blindingly dusty streets of summer, board-walks put down on the pavements every winter . . . and the dreadful college bell reverberant over all.' (Aiken, 1952).

Eliot is introduced into Boston society by his uncle, Christopher Rhodes Eliot, a prominent Unitarian minister. In 1918, in his article 'The Hawthorne Aspect of Henry James', Eliot will describe his first impressions of Boston society; poems such as 'The Boston Evening Transcript', 'Aunt Helen', and 'Cousin Nancy', later suggest that Eliot takes a satirical view of its conventionality.

Eliot's undergraduate programme consists of 18 courses, including (in his first year) 7 classical courses, French and German, medieval history, English and comparative literature, and history of modern philosophy. Eliot also attends classes in Dante's *Divine Comedy*; students have no prior knowledge of Italian, but use a prose translation in conjunction with the text. Eliot steeps himself in Dante's poetry, reciting it to himself lying in bed or on a railway journey, (Smidt, 1949) and Dante becomes a lasting influence on his poetry and thought. Eliot also takes courses in the poetry of John Donne, which he will recall in 1931 in his article, 'Donne in Our Time'.

1907

24 May: Eliot's poem, 'Song: When We came Home across the Hill' is printed in the *Harvard Advocate*, the university's literary magazine.

28 May: K. G. T. Webster, an assistant instructor in comparative literature, reviews the poem in *The Crimson*: 'Mr Eliot's "Song" is pretty and suggestive in its vague way. In general, *Advocate* poets — as well as others — should consider that sense hurts no poem.'

3 June: Eliot's 'Song: If Space and Time, as Sages say' (slightly altered from 'A Lyric' printed in the *Smith Academy Record* in April 1905) is printed in the *Harvard Advocate*.

1908

13 November: Eliot's poem 'Before Morning' appears in the *Harvard Advocate*. B.A.G. Fuller reviews it in *The Crimson*: 'One is jolted, not impressed.'

25 November: Eliot's poem 'Circe's Palace' appears in the *Harvard Advocate*.

December: In the library of the Harvard Union Eliot discovers a copy of Arthur Symons's *The Symbolist Movement in Literature* (1899). The book introduces Eliot to the work of the French Symbolist poets Rimbaud, Verlaine, Mallarmé, and, most importantly, Laforgue; whose impact on his poetry Eliot will describe in his 1919 article, 'Reflections on Contemporary Poetry'. The results of this new influence will first be seen in the poems published in the *Harvard Advocate* in November 1909 and January 1910.

In 1946, in his *Poetry* article, 'Ezra Pound', Eliot will describe the intellectual climate of Harvard in 1908.

1909

January: Eliot continues his studies in Latin literature with a course on the Roman novel, in which he studies Petronius' *Satyricon*, later used in epigraphs to *The Waste Land* and *The Sacred Wood*.

26 January: Eliot's 'Song: The Moonflower opens to the Moth' and 'On a Portrait' are printed in the *Harvard Advocate*.

7 May: Eliot is appointed to the board of editors of the *Harvard Advocate*.

June: Eliot completes his undergraduate course (AB) at Harvard.

July/August: Eliot spends the summer at the family house near East Gloucester.

October: Eliot returns to Harvard for an MA course in English Literature. One of his courses is Irving Babbitt's 'Literary Criticism in France with Special Reference to the Nineteenth Century'. Babbitt's course and recently published book, *Literature and the American College* (1908), introduce Eliot to the theory of the living past and the value of tradition. Babbitt wrote that the supremacy of Greek literature had lain in 'the balance it maintained between the forces of tradition and claims of originality' – one of the major themes of Eliot's later critical work. In October 1933, Eliot will write in *The Criterion* of his impressions of Babbitt.

Eliot's programme also includes George Santayana's course, 'The Philosophy of History: Ideals of Society, Religion, Art and Science in their Historical Development'. Some of the material from the course is incorporated into Santayana's *Three Philosophical Poets: Lucretius, Dante and Goethe* (1910), from which one phrase describing *The Divine Comedy* ('it all ends, not with a bang, not with some casual incident, but in sustained reflection . . . ') finds an echo in the final couplet of Eliot's 'The Hollow Men' (1925).

12 November: Eliot's 'Nocturne', his first poem to show the influence of Laforgue, is printed in the *Harvard Advocate*. The tone of the poem – witty, detached, anti-heroic – looks forward to 'The Love Song of J. Alfred Prufrock' and echoes Symons's description of Laforgue: 'He composes love-poems hat in hand, and smiles with an exasperating tolerance before all the transformations of the eternal feminine. . .He will not permit, at any moment, the luxury of dropping the mask.' (Symons, 1899).

1910

12 January: Eliot's poem, 'Humouresque', subtitled '(After J. Laforgue)', is printed in the *Harvard Advocate*.

26 January: Eliot's poem, 'Spleen', is printed in the *Harvard Advocate*.

3 April: Eliot's mother writes to him about a proposed plan that he should spend the following year pursuing his studies at the Sorbonne in Paris. (Gordon, 1977).

24 June: Eliot graduates from Harvard. His 'Ode: For the Hour that is left us, Fair Harvard, with thee', written to commemorate the occasion, is printed in the *Harvard Advocate*, and reprinted on the same day in *The Boston Evening Transcript* and *The Boston Evening Herald*.

July/August: During his summer vacation at East Gloucester, Eliot buys a marbled notebook from the Old Corner Bookstore, entitles it *Inventions of the March Hare*, and copies into it all his more experimental poems written since November 1909, omitting the earlier poems published in the *Harvard Advocate*. He continues to use this notebook during the following year in Paris.

September/October: Eliot arrives in Paris to spend a year at the Sorbonne. He settles at no. 9 rue de l'Université, a pension on the left bank.

At some time during 1910 Eliot writes the first two 'Preludes', the first part of 'The Love Song of J. Alfred Prufrock' (to be completed in 1911). and 'Portrait of a Lady' whose source Conrad Aiken describes (Aiken, 1952) as being a *précieuse ridicule* in Boston society.

In June 1935, in an article in the *New English Weekly*, Eliot will comment on the American intellectual climate of 1910.

1910-11

During the academic year 1910–11 Eliot attends lectures at the Sorbonne, goes to the Collège de France to hear Henri Bergson's weekly philosophy lectures, and is taught French by Alain-Fournier, then working on his novel *Le Grand Meaulnes* (1913). He buys the periodicals *Cahiers de la Quinzaine*, and the *Nouvelle Revue Francaise*, and will continue to subscribe to the latter when he returns to Harvard. He also reads *Bubu de Montparnasse*, a popular novel of the Paris underworld, by Charles-Louis Philippe; and its images of urban decay and poverty influence his poetry of this time, as well as 'The Waste Land'. When the novel is reprinted in 1932 Eliot will write a preface to it.

During this period Eliot is visited in Paris by Conrad Aiken, who recalls (Aiken, 1952): 'the first visit to the *pâtisserie* and then *sirop de fraises* and soda at the sidewalk café'. Eliot also befriends a young Frenchman, Jean Verdenal, a medical student and poet, killed in World War I, to whom in 1917 he will dedicate *Prufrock and Other Observations*.

Eliot's year in Paris, recalled in *The Criterion* of April 1934, has a lasting influence on his thought, stimulating his already strong interest in French poetry, introducing him, through the *Nouvelle Revue Francaise*, to the thought of Charles Maurras, the Roman Catholic scholar, and forming him into a critic and editor always conscious that British culture is part of a European tradition.

1911

April: Eliot's holograph poem, 'Interlude in London' suggests he made a brief visit to England. (Gordon, 1977).

July/August: Eliot travels in Europe, visiting northern Italy and Munich. During this period he finishes the third 'Prelude' and the final version of 'The Love Song of J. Alfred Prufrock'. Eliot will later recall (letter to *The Times Literary Supplement*, 8 July 1960) that he made additions to 'Prufrock' in 1912, but later removed them, at Conrad Aiken's suggestion.

September/October: Eliot returns to Harvard to read for a doctorate in philosophy. Conrad Aiken recalls (1952) that he found Eliot 'perceptibly Europeanized'. He also recalls the popular cartoon strips the two young men enjoyed — Krazy Kat, Mutt and Jeff, the work of Rube Goldberg — and that they discussed the possibility of making their lives in Europe.

Eliot enrols in Lanman's Indic philology course, studies Sanskrit and Pali, and reads Indian philosophy under James Haughton Woods, he also teaches some undergraduate courses. In 1946, in his broadcast 'The Unity of European Culture' Eliot will recall his studies in Indian philosophy.

1912

Eliot is absorbed in his philosophical studies; Kristian Smidt reports (1949) that in conversation Eliot said they *were* him at this time. In 1912 the book *New Realism*, by E. B. Holt and others, made a great impression on American philosophical studies. The Six Realists, co-authors of the book, expressing themselves broadly in agreement with Bertrand Russell and other Cambridge philosophers, stressed the pre-eminence of science and felt that: 'the mathematician was the man best qualified to philosophize'. (Eliot, 1952). In the *New English Weekly* of 6 June 1935, and in his preface to Joseph Pieper's *Leisure as the Basis of Culture* (1952), Eliot will express his own disassociation from this line of thought.

That Eliot is also working intermittently on his poetry is suggested by a letter to *The Times Literary Supplement* of 8 July 1960, in which he recalls that he made additions to 'The Love Song of J. Alfred Prufrock' in 1912, but, at Conrad Aiken's suggestion, later removed them.

1913

17 February: Eliot acts in a variety show in the Cambridge house of his aunt, Mrs. Holmes Hinkley. He plays Mr Woodhouse in a scene from Jane Austen's *Emma* and Monsieur Marcel in a sketch, 'Monsieur Marcel and his latest Marvel', devised by his cousin, Eleanor Hinkley. Her friend, Emily Hale, plays Mrs Elton. Various commentators have suggested that Eliot fell in love with Emily Hale. She never married and became a teacher of drama, over the course of her life exchanging about 2000 letters with Eliot (at present to be kept in Princeton University until 2020). Later he renews contact with her, when he visits the USA in 1933 and she visits England for two successive summers in 1934 and 1935.

March: The *Nouvelle Revue Francaise*, to which Eliot continues to subscribe, carries a study of Charles Maurras by Albert Thibaudet, with a footnote describing Maurras' three traditions as 'classique, catholique, monarchique'. In the preface to *For Lancelot Andrews* (1928), Eliot will echo these three traditions in a description of his own line of thought.

Spring: Eliot withdraws from the Sanskrit courses. In 1933, in his Virginia lectures (published in 1934 as *After Strange Gods*), Eliot will describe his difficulties in studying Sanskrit and explain his reasons for leaving the courses.

June: Eliot buys F. H. Bradley's *Appearance and Reality* (1893), probably reads it over the summer vacation, and decides that the subject of his doctoral dissertation will be the epistemology of F. H. Bradley. Its final title is *Meinong's Gegenstandstheorie considered in relation to Bradley's Theory of Knowledge* and it will be published in 1964 as *Knowledge and Experience in the Philosophy of F. H. Bradley*.

October: Eliot is appointed president of the university philosophical club for the academic year 1913/14.

9 December: Eliot reads a class report on primitive religions. He criticizes some anthropologists — Frazer, Jane Harrison, Durkheim and Levy-Bruhl — for giving no explanation of religious ritual 'in terms of need'. (Gordon, 1977).

16 December: Again in a class report, Eliot tries to by-pass anthropologists' records of behaviour with the question: 'What is he (the believer) sincere about?' Behaviour is mere mechanism, Eliot adds, unless it has some sort of meaning: 'The question is, what is that meaning?' (Gordon, 1977).

1914

January/February: Eliot is awarded a Sheldon Travelling Fellowship to pursue his studies for one year in England, at Oxford University.

24 February: In a class report, Eliot criticizes all theories of knowledge for their inability to 'treat illusion as real'. Lyndall Gordon suggests that at this time Eliot is hovering on the edge of conversion, a supposition based on a group of religious poems composed during this period, but never published. These include the 'Death of St Narcissus', later used by Eliot in the first draft of 'The Waste Land', but edited out by Ezra Pound.

27 March: Bertrand Russell, a visiting lecturer at Harvard during the spring term, describes in a letter to Lady Ottoline Morrell how that morning two of his pupils had come to see him, one of them being Eliot.

In his *Autobiography* (1967) Russell recalls Eliot as a pupil in his post-graduate class: 'I was praising Heraclitus, and he (Eliot) observed: "Yes, he always reminds me of Villon". I thought this remark so good I always wished he would make another.'

(Eliot's poem, 'Mr. Apollinax', is a disguised portrait of Russell.)

May: In a letter to Lady Ottoline Morrell, Russell mentions a weekend party at which Eliot was present. Russell describes Eliot as 'ultra-civilised'.

Early June: Eliot leaves Harvard to travel, via Paris and Munich, to the University of Marburg in Germany to attend the lectures of Rudolf Eucken, the German philosopher.

July/August: Eliot arrives at Marburg, where he stays about a fortnight. During this time, World War I breaks out in Europe.

Late August: Eliot arrives in London. His friend, Conrad Aiken, has already spent the summer there and tried, without success, to find a publisher for Eliot's poetry to date. (In a letter to *The Times Literary Supplement* of 8 July 1960, Eliot recalls that Aiken tried Harold Munro, editor of *Poetry and Drama*, and Austin Harrison of the *English Review* 'amongst others'.) Eliot Finds that Aiken has returned to the USA but has left him an introduction to Ezra Pound, the American poet and critic, founder of the Imagist movement in painting, whose many involvements in literary journalism include acting as London correspondent of the Chicago-based *Poetry* magazine. Pound finds the magazine conventional and slow to recognise new talent, and conducts much quarrelsome correspondence with its editor, Harriet Monroe.

22 September: Eliot calls to see Pound at his flat in Kensington.

30 September: Pound writes to Harriet Monroe, praising a poem that Eliot has sent him ('The Love Song of J. Alfred Prufrock').

October: Pound again writes to Harriet Monroe, enclosing 'The Love Song of J. Alfred Prufrock'. He urges her to publish it in *Poetry* as soon as possible.

Bertrand Russell meets Eliot by accident in New Oxford Street. They discuss the war, and Eliot tells Russell that he is 'not a pacifist' (Russell, 1967).

Eliot arrives at Merton College, Oxford, to complete his thesis on F. H. Bradley. Eliot's tutor, Harold Joachim, is an ex-colleague and pupil of Bradley's. Eliot also studies Aristotle, going to Joachim's lectures on Aristotle's Nicomachean Ethics (published posthumously in book form, 1951). Eliot will pay tribute to Joachim in *The Times*, August 1938; and will briefly recall war-time Oxford in his preface to *A Memorial Volume to Aldous Huxley* (1965).

9 November: Pound writes two letters to Harriet Monroe, rejecting some criticisms she has made on 'The Love Song of J. Alfred Prufrock'.

1915

Early 1915:   The painter and writer, Wyndham Lewis, collecting material for the second edition of his literary magazine *Blast*, writes to Pound that Eliot has sent him 'Bullshit' and 'The Ballad for Big Louise', which Lewis calls 'two excellent bits of scholarly ribaldry'. Bernard Bergonzi suggests (1972) that they may have been part of an unpublished saga about a figure called King Bolo — humorous, mildly obscene doggerel that Eliot worked on intermittently for years. Eliot's talent for light verse will also be demonstrated in *Old Possum's Book of Practical Cats* (1939).

January: During Eliot's Christmas vacation from Merton College, he spends some time at Swanage, Dorset, with two other young Americans. Eliot reads A. N. Whitehead's and Bertrand Russell's *Principia Mathematica* (1910).

31 January: In a letter to Harriet Monroe, Pound again defends Eliot's 'The Love Song of J. Alfred Prufrock' and says that Eliot would not agree to deletion of the 'Hamlet' paragraph. He assures Harriet Monroe that 'Prufrock' is the best poem of Eliot's that he has seen; and that Eliot is 'quite *intelligent* . . . '

25 February: Eliot writes to Conrad Aiken that Harvard has renominated him to his Fellowship, but that he does not enjoy Oxford. He would like to continue his studies in the British Museum in London, though he does not think he would ever come to like England; on the other hand, he is unwilling to return to Harvard. (Bergonzi, 1972).

10 April: Pound finishes a letter to Harriet Monroe with: '*Do* get on with that Eliot.'

26 April: Eliot mentions in a letter a girl called 'Vivienne'. During the summer term Eliot dances and goes punting with Vivienne Haigh-Wood, at that time a governess with a Cambridge family. Vivienne was, like Eliot, born in 1888. Her father was a distinguished etcher and painter of private means, and she had one brother eight years younger than herself.

June: 'The Love Song of J. Alfred Prufrock' is printed in *Poetry* magazine.

26 June: One week after the end of Oxford's Trinity term, Eliot and Vivienne Haigh-Wood are married in Hampstead registry office, with two friends of Vivienne's as witnesses.

July: Bertrand Russell recalls in his *Autobiography* (1967) that he dined

Prufrock completed in 1912, through the help of Ezra Pound it is published in Poetry magazine in 1915

9

with Eliot and his new bride: 'an artist I think he said, but I should have thought her an actress.'

The second number of *Blast* appears, containing the 'Preludes' and 'Rhapsody on a Windy Night', the first British publication of any of Eliot's work.

At about this time, Eliot returns to the USA to see his father, who, disapproving of his son's decision to settle in England and forego an academic career, refuses to continue his allowance.

September: Eliot's poem 'Portrait of a Lady' is printed in the American magazine *Others*, a competitor to *Poetry*.

10 September: Eliot writes to his father expressing his worries about money and justifying his decision to stay in England. (Valerie Eliot, 1971).

25 September: Pound writes to Harriet Monroe that Eliot is back in England, and that Harold Munro, editor of *Poetry and Drama*, who had previously rejected Eliot's work, has been expressing his interest in the author of 'Prufrock'.

September/October: Eliot and his wife move to Bertrand Russell's flat, Russell having agreed to let them a room.

Robert Sencourt suggests that Vivienne Eliot and Bertrand Russell, at that time a notorious exponent of 'free love', had a brief affair. However, Russell and Eliot continue to be on friendly terms, though in 1927 Eliot will state that one of the reasons for his conversion to Anglicanism was a recoil from Russell's agnosticism. (Sencourt, 1971).

Eliot takes up a teaching job for one term at High Wycombe Grammer School, at a salary of £140 p.a.

October: 'Three Poems' by Eliot, 'The Boston Evening Transcript', 'Aunt Helen' and 'Cousin Nancy', are printed in *Poetry* magazine. *The Egoist* magazine, of which in 1917 Eliot is to become assistant editor, comments on this issue: 'Miss Monroe has the able assistance of. . .Mr Ezra Pound. One of their latest discoveries is Mr T. S. Eliot, also printed in *Blast*, whose poetry has an individual flavour.'

2 October: Pound writes to Harriet Monroe about the Helen Hair Levinson Prize for poetry, worth $200, saying that he has voted for Eliot. (It is awarded, in December, to the American poet Vachel Lindsay.)

10 November: Bertrand Russell writes to Lady Ottoline Morrell about the Eliots, describing Vivienne as: 'a person who lives on a knife-edge'.

Vivienne's health, both physical and mental, is always fragile; and its progressive deterioration during her marriage to Eliot adds greatly to his mental tension, as well as to his financial responsibilities.

Late November: The *Catholic Anthology*, a collection of modern poetry, is published, edited by Pound. It contains 'Prufrock', 'Portrait of a Lady', 'The Boston Evening Transcript', 'Miss Helen Slingsby' and 'Hysteria' — the first appearance in book form of any of Eliot's poetry. Other contributors include W. B. Yeats. The book is denounced by Arthur Waugh, a leading conservative critic, in *The Quarterly Review*: 'the unmetrical incoherent banalities of these literary "Cubists".'

December: Vivienne's health deteriorates, and she collapses.

1 December: In a letter to Harriet Monroe, Pound again defends 'Prufrock', saying that it is 'more individual and unusual' than 'Portrait of a Lady'. He tells Monroe that he is sending her some more of Eliot's poetry; and mentions that Eliot has a job in London for the following year.

1916

January: A review by Eliot of A. J. Balfour's *Theism and Humanism* appears in the Chicago philosophy periodical, the *International Journal of Ethics*. Eliot becomes a regular reviewer for the *Journal*.

10 January: Eliot writes to Conrad Aiken, telling him of Vivienne's ill-health, and of the death of Jean Verdenal; and regretting that the *Catholic* Anthology has not sold more copies. He says that he hopes to be able to resume his own writing. 'I have lived through material for a score of long poems in the last six months.' (Valerie Eliot, 1971).

Mid-January: Bertrand Russell takes Vivienne to convalesce in Torquay, while Eliot remains in London. He takes up a teaching post at Highgate Junior School, north London, at a salary of £160 pa, and stays till the end of 1916. The poet John Betjeman, a pupil at the school, recalls in *Summoned by Bells* (1960) presenting 'the American master' with a volume of juvenile verse — received by Eliot with marked lack of enthusiasm.

January/February: Eliot completes his doctoral dissertation and sends a copy to Harvard. His former teacher, James Haughton Woods, receives it favourably and reports that the department of philosophy has accepted it without hesitation and that Josiah Royce has called it 'the work of an expert'. Woods adds: Please let us be reassured that your interest in Philosophy is as strong as ever.' (Gordon, 1977). Eliot plans to sail to the USA to take the oral examinations necessary for his doctorate; he also plans, at the request of Ezra Pound, to transport some Vorticist paintings to New York for an exhibition. However, Eliot never makes the journey, probably due to lack of funds and the danger presented by German submarines. Nor does he ever receive his doctorate, but it will be published in 1964 under the title *Knowledge and Experience in the Philosophy of F. H. Bradley*.

21 April: In a letter to Harriet Monroe, Pound mentions a book that Eliot is planning. The book is to become *Prufrock and Other Observations*.

May: Eliot's mother writes to Bertrand Russell, urging him to encourage Eliot to concentrate on philosophy, rather than poetry writing, as a 'life-work'. (Russell, 1967).

June/July: Bertrand Russell asks Clive Bell to befriend Eliot (March and Tambimuttu, 1948). Through Bell, Eliot comes into contact with Roger Fry, Leonard and Virginia Woolf, Lytton Strachey and Lowes Dickinson. Bell also introduces Eliot into Ottoline Morrell's circle, where he meets Aldous Huxley and Middleton Murry.

July: In a letter to Wyndham Lewis, Pound describes a weekend party at the seaside which included Eliot, Roger Fry and Lowes Dickinson.

21 August: Eliot writes to Conrad Aiken about his reviewing work: 'It is good practice in writing, and teaches one speed both in reading and writing.' (Valerie Eliot, 1971). He adds that he is trying to get an introduction to *The Nation*.

September: Four poems by Eliot are printed in *Poetry* under the heading *Observations*: 'Conversation galante', 'La figlia che piange', 'Mr. Apollinax' and 'Morning at the Window'.

Eliot begins a series of six lectures on Modern French Literature and sixteen lectures on Modern English Literature, for extension courses at Oxford and the University of London respectively.

6 September: Eliot writes to his brother telling him how difficult the year he has been, and that he feels that 'Prufrock' might be a 'swan-song'. (Valerie Eliot, 1971).

October: In the *International Journal of Ethics*, Eliot reviews *Conscience and Christ*, by the Oxford theologian Hastings Rashdall, and *Group Theories of Religion and the Religion of the Individual*, by another Oxford don, Clement Webb. Eliot comments dryly on the 'modern methods' of Christianity expounded by both writers.

Having been introduced by Bertrand Russell to Philip Jourdain, the British correspondent of the *Monist*, another Chicago-based periodical, Eliot contributes two highly technical articles on Leibnitz to the October issue: *The Development of Leivniz's Monadism*, in which Eliot finds two currents in Leibniz's thought, his scientific evolution and his devotion to theology; and *Leibniz's Monads and Bradley's Finite Centers*, in which he traces links between Leibniz's and Bradley's thought. (Both essays are reprinted as appendices to *Knowledge and Experience in the Philosophy of F. H. Bradley*, 1964).

6 November: Eliot writes to his brother Henry that he is giving up teaching at the end of the year. (Valerie Eliot, 1971). He will later tell Walter Turner Levy (Levy and Scherle, 1968) that he found the work so demanding that he had no energy left for his own writing, even during the long vacation.

29 December: Aldous Huxley writes to his brother Julian, recommending him to read Eliot's poems.

During 1916, Eliot also reviews books for the *New Statesman* and the *Manchester Guardian*.

1917

January: Ezra Pound writes to Margaret Anderson, editor and founder of the American literary periodical, *The Little Review*, recommending Eliot as a critic and contributor.

March: Pound writes to Alice Corbin Henderson, co-editor of *Poetry*, suggesting that he, Eliot and the French critic Jean de Bosschère write a series on French poets for the magazine.

3 March: Eliot's article, 'Reflections on Vers Libre', appears in the *New Statesman*: 'The division between Conservative Verse and *vers libre* does not exist, for there is only good verse, bad verse, and chaos.'

19 March: Following an introduction by Vivienne's family, Eliot starts work with the Colonial and Foreign Department of Lloyds Bank in Queen Victoria Street, where he will stay for nine years. His work at first involves him in settling pre-war enemy debts, then with the bank's Foreign Information Bureau. *Vivienne's family got him the job*

6 April: The USA enters World War I. Eliot has already offered his services to the American navy, but has been refused on account of a boyhood hernia.

11 April: Pound writes to John Quinn, his New York lawyer and a patron of the arts, that Elkin Matthews, publisher of the *Catholic Anthology*, is reluctant to publish Eliot's new book, and that *The Egoist* will publish it, Pound having borrowed the cost of the printing bill.

May: Pound becomes foreign editor of *The Little Review*. In the May issue Eliot's 'Eeldrop and Appleplex', a piece of humorous prose, is published; in July the magazine will print four poems of his. In May 1929 Eliot will pay tribute to the magazine for being the only American periodical which would publish his work, at this time.

June: Eliot becomes assistant editor of *The Egoist*, replacing Richard Aldington, who has enlisted. *The Egoist* was started in 1913 by Harriet Weaver as *The New Freewoman*, an organ of philosophical feminism. Pound had been in charge of the literary section, which provided a platform for the Imagists and their friends. In *The Egoist* Eliot will develop his critical ideas in a series of reviews of modern English, American and French poetry; he will also publish a serialization of the early chapters of James Joyce's *Ulysses*.

Eliot's *Prufrock and Other Observations* is published by the Egoist Press Ltd. in an edition of 500 copies, price one shilling. It contains 12 poems already printed in various periodicals and in the *Catholic Anthology*. Eliot will later (*Encounter*, 1962) pay tribute to Harriet Weaver's readiness to bring out the book, doubting that it would otherwise have found a publisher. The book attracts mixed critical response; *The Times Literary Supplement* is dismissive, but the *Westminster Gazette* sees Eliot as: 'A poet who finds even poetry laughable, who views life with a dry derision and comments on it with the true disengagement of wit'; and the *New Statesman* comments: 'Mr. Eliot may possibly give us the quintessence of twenty-first century poetry'. Clive Bell recalls (March and Tambimuttu, 1948) taking copies to a weekend party at Lady Ottoline Morrell's house at Garsington, where: 'it caused a stir, much discussion, some perplexity.'

In the June issue of *The Egoist*, Pound defends Eliot against Arthur Waugh's attack on the *Catholic Anthology* (see November 1915): '*I have tried to write of a few things that have really moved me*, is, so far as I know, the sum of Mr. Eliot's "poetic theory".'

July: *The Little Review* publishes Eliot's poems 'Le Directeur', 'Mélange Adultère de Tout', 'Lune de Miel', and 'The Hippopotamus'. The latter poem is the first in a series of 'quatrain' poems which mark a change in Eliot's style, of which Pound will give an account in *The Criterion*, July 1932. The other 'quatrain' poems are 'Sweeney Among the Nightingales', 'Whispers of Immortality', 'Mr. Eliot's Sunday Morning Service', 'A Cooking Egg', 'Burbank with a Baedeker: Bleistein with a Cigar', and 'Sweeney Erect'.

26 August: Pound writes to Harriet Monroe about a proposed series of articles on French poetry, to which Eliot is supposed to be contributing. Pound comments that Eliot's work at the bank leaves him even less free for his own work than before.

September: Eliot gives the first of 25 lectures on Victorian Literature at the County Secondary School, Sydenham. He is also preparing a lecture course on 'The Makers of Nineteenth-Century Ideas'.

Autumn: Herbert Read, later the distinguished art historian but at this time a soldier on leave from the front, recalls (Tate, 1967) meeting Eliot in London to discuss Eliot contributing to a new magazine, *Art and Letters*. Read describes Eliot as: 'a very modest young man of twenty-nine, dressed correctly in a dark city suit'.

October and November: Eliot writes to his mother, telling her of his relief that enough students have enrolled for both of his courses; and also saying that his wife, Vivienne, has been looking for a job but is hampered by her continual ill-health. (Valerie Eliot, 1971).

December: In the December issue of *The Egoist* Eliot contributes five letters parodying different literary styles and opinions. They are signed: Charles Augustus Coneybeare of the Carlton Club, Liverpool; the Reverend Charles James Grimble of the Vicarage, Leays; J. A. D. Spench, (a master at Thridlingston Grammar School); Muriel A. Schwarz of Hampstead; and Helen B. Troundlett.

11 December: In a letter to Juliette Baillot Huxley mentions that Eliot is 'haggard and ill-looking as usual'.

12 December: Eliot and Huxley take part in a charity poetry reading organized by Sybil Colefax, the society hostess. Other participants include the Sitwells. The audience includes the novelist Arnold Bennett, who later recalls (Bennett, 1932) that he was so struck by Eliot's work that he made his acquaintance.

During 1917 Eliot continues to review for the *International Journal of Ethics* and the *New Statesman*.

1918

January: Eliot's article, 'In Memory of Henry James', is printed in *The Egoist*; James had: 'a mind so fine that no *idea* could violate it'.

A bound pamphlet on Pound's work, *Ezra Pound: His Metric and Poetry*, written anonymously by Eliot, is published by Knopf in New York. Its purpose is to introduce Pound to a larger American public and to accompany a collection of Pound's poems and translations from the Japanese Noh drama. Eliot stresses that Pound's work must be read in chronological order: the reader is only ready for 'The Cantos' when he has read 'Lustra' and 'Cathay'.

23 March: Eliot's first review in *The Nation* is printed, unsigned; on Bertrand Russell's *Mysticism and Logic*. Eliot compares Russell's prose to that of F. H. Bradley's.

19 April: Eliot writes to John Quinn that he regrets not being able to increase the size of *Prufrock and Other Observations* to make it suitable for American publication. He explains that his work at Lloyds Bank and on *The Egoist*, and his evening lectures, leave him little energy for his own writing. (Valerie Eliot, 1971).

10 May: Eliot writes to his mother about the possibility of one of his courses of evening lectures being on Elizabethan literature; expressing his interest in eventually writing some essays on the Elizabethan dramatists. (Valerie Eliot, 1971).

June/July: Eliot's doctor advises that he and Vivienne should spend the summer out of London, and Bertrand Russell lends them his house at Marlow, Buckinghamshire.

9 June: Eliot writes to his mother from Marlow (Valerie Eliot, 1971) that he is feeling better; and that he is writing an article on Henry James and Hawthorne (to be published in August).

While at Marlow the Eliots are visited by Aldous Huxley, then a master at nearby Eton (described by Huxley in a letter to his brother Julian, 28 June).

August: Eliot's article, 'The Hawthorn Aspect of Henry James' is published in *The Little Review*. Eliot describes Boston society — which he himself knew as a student — as: 'Quite uncivilised. . .but refined beyond the point of civilisation'.

August/September: Eliot makes renewed attempts to enlist, applying to the Intelligence Services of first the American navy, then the army. At one point he resigns from Lloyds Bank, only to return two weeks later. Eventually he reports to John Quinn: 'Everything turned to red tape in my hands.' (Valerie Eliot, 1971).

September: Eliot gives the first of 18 lectures in Elizabethan literature, at the County Secondary School, Sydenham.

The Little Review publishes Eliot's poems 'Sweeney Among the Nightingales', 'Whispers of Immortality', 'Dans le Restaurant' and 'Mr. Eliot's Sunday Morning Service'.

Eliot reviews Wyndham Lewis's novel *Tarr* in *The Egoist*. He says of *Tarr* and Joyce's *Ulysses*: 'Both are terrifying. That is the test of a new work of art.'

8 September: Eliot writes to Quinn, telling him he has almost finished preparing a selection of poems and prose, to be sent to the USA for consideration by the American publishers, Knopf. (Valerie Eliot, 1971).

15 November: Eliot makes his first visit to Leonard and Virginia Woolf at Hogarth House, Richmond, taking some poems which he hopes the Woolfs will publish. The poems are accepted by the Woolfs and will be published in May 1919.

December: Ezra Pound writes to the American poet Marianne Moore about the contributions he is receiving for *The Little Review*; saying he is rejecting imitators of Eliot.

During 1918, Eliot reviews books regularly in the *New Statesman* and the *International Journal of Ethics*.

1919

Early 1919:   Middleton Murry takes over the editorship of *The Athenaeum*, London's august literary and critical weekly. Murry invites Eliot to become assistant editor and contributor, along with the Woolfs, Lytton Strachey, Clive Bell and Roger Fry. Eliot reviews for *The Athenaeum* regularly during the year; and will recall (in his foreword to Murry's *Katherine Mansfield and Other Literary Studies*, 1959) that the period when Murry was editor of *The Athenaeum* and Bruce Richmond was editor of *The Times Literary Supplement* was 'the high summer of literary journalism in my life-time'.

8 January: Eliot's father, Henry Ware Eliot, dies.

29 March: Eliot writes to his mother that he has declined Murry's offer of the assistant editorship of *The Athenaeum*. (Valerie Eliot, 1971).

25 April: In a review in *The Athenaeum* of *A History of American Literature*, Eliot writes on Hawthorne, Poe and Whitman, and on the dilemma of the American writer generally: 'The originality, if not the full mental capability, of these men was brought out, forced out, by the starved environment . . . Their world was thin; it was not corrupt enough.'

29 April: John Quinn writes to Eliot telling him that Knopf would be interested in publishing the poems Eliot had sent him, but not the prose. (Valerie Eliot, 1971).

1 May: Eliot's poem, 'A Cooking Egg' is published in *Coterie*, a new illustrated quarterly.

12 May: Eliot's *Poems* is published by Hogarth Press. Leonard Woolf recalls in *Beginning Again* (1964): 'Of Tom's *Poems* we printed rather fewer than 250 copies. We published it in May 1919 price 2s 6d and it went out of print in the middle of 1920.'

25 May: Eliot writes to John Quinn that he would like to add a few more poems (including 'Gerontion') and essays to the selection he has sent to Knopf. (Valerie Eliot, 1971).

Summer: Eliot's poems, 'Burbank with a Baedeker: Bleistein with a Cigar', and 'Sweeney Erect' are published in the quarterly *Art and Letters*, edited by Frank Rutter and Herbert Read (anonymously by the latter, as his work at the Treasury precludes him from engaging in any journalistic activities).

1 June: Eliot writes to the essayist Lytton Strachey about the process of his writing; also describing his work in the provinces for Lloyds Bank. (Holroyd, 1967). Strachey describes this letter as 'grim'.

July: Eliot's article, 'Reflections on Contemporary Poetry', appears in *The Egoist*. Eliot discusses how a young writer may suddenly fall under the spell of an older one, and through him become part of a literary tradition. Commenting implicitly on his own discovery of Jules Laforgue in 1908, Eliot describes: 'a feeling of profound kinship, or rather of a peculiar personal intimacy, with another, probably a dead author'.

August: Eliot goes on a walking holiday in the Dordogne, France; briefly described in a postcard to Lytton Strachey. (Holroyd, 1967).

September: The first part of one of Eliot's most famous essays, 'Tradition and the Individual Talent', appears in the penultimate issue of *The Egoist*. Speaking of literary tradition, Eliot says that it: 'involves, in the first place, the historical sense. . .and the historical sense involves a perception, not only of the pastness of the past, but of its presence; the historical sense compels a man to write not merely with his own generation in his bones, but with a feeling that the whole of the literature of Europe from Homer

17

and within it the whole of the literature of his own country has a simultaneous existence and composes a simultaneous order.'

In this and other reviews published in *The Athenaeum* on 26 September and 17 October, Eliot seems to be referring to his own poetic technique in 'The Waste Land', probably germinating in his mind at this time.

26 September: A review by Eliot of J. M. Robertson's *The Problem of 'Hamlet'* is printed in *The Athenaeum*. Eliot proposes the concept of an 'objective correlative' as a tool of poetic technique: 'such that when the external facts, which must terminate in sensory experience, are given, the emotion is immediately evoked'.

17 October: A review by Eliot in *The Athenaeum*, of *The Path of the Rainbow*, indicates Eliot's growing interest in primitive art and poetry, and their power to 'revivify the contemporary activities'. This line of thought will soon reappear in Eliot's use of two books of anthropology, *From Ritual to Romance* by Jessie Weston (1920) and *The Golden Bough* by J. M. Frazer (1890) in 'The Waste Land'.

5 November: Eliot writes to John Quinn, thanking him for sending Knopf's contract; Knopf having agreed to publish Eliot's poems without the prose, under the title *Poems by T. S. Eliot*. Eliot adds that when he has finished an article for *The Times Literary Supplement*: 'I hope to get started on a poem I have in mind.' (Valerie Eliot, 1971). This is his first mention of the poem that is to become 'The Waste Land'.

13 November: Eliot's review of *Ben Jonson*, by G. Gregory Smith, appears (unsigned) in *The Times Literary Supplement*; Eliot's first review for this publication. Eliot will recall Bruce Richmond, its editor, in his preface to *Katherine Mansfield and Other Literary Studies* (1959), and in his tribute to Richmond in *The Times* of 13 January 1961.

December: *Coterie* contains a parody by Robert Nichols of Eliot's quatrain poems:

> Sinclair's looks can never lie,
> He is well shaved, has curved lips,
> His nose is straight, so is his eye,
> Also he boasts substantial hips.

> Sinclair would make his muslin choice —
> Spring and his father say he must:
> Corah has ankles and a voice,
> Nancy has French and a neat bust.

Similar imitations by other poets appeared in later issues.

1920

Early February: Eliot's book of poetry, *Ara Vos Prec*, is published by The Ovid Press. The title, three words in Provencal meaning 'Now I pray you' comes from canto XXVI of Dante's *Purgatorio*, later alluded to in 'The Waste Land' and 'Ash-Wednesday'.

12 February: *The Times Literary Supplement* records the publication of *Ara Vos Prec*: 'Verses by an able scholar and littérateur — whose poetical work, however, may be said to be the most challenging and bizarre of any of the younger bands of the day.'

15 February: In a letter to his brother Eliot says that he thinks 'Sweeney Among the Nightingales' and 'Burbank' are some of the best work that he has done. He fears that, whilst in England he is considered 'a wit or satirist': 'in America I suppose I shall be thought merely disgusting'. (Valerie Eliot, 1971).

Late February: *Poems by T. S. Eliot* is published by Knopf in New York; Eliot's first American publication in book form.

18 March: *The Times Literary Supplement* reviews *Ara Vos Prec*: 'Again and again he (Eliot) tells us that he is "fed-up" with art, with life, with people, with things. . .Mr. Eliot does not convince us that his weariness is anything but a habit, an anti-romantic tradition . . . which he must throw off.'

26 March: Eliot writes to Quinn, telling him he is compiling a book of essays (published in November as *The Sacred Wood*); and saying he hopes to find a 'good publisher'. (Valerie Eliot, 1971).

10 April: The London publishers Methuen contract with Eliot for publication of 'a volume of essays'.

14 May: In an *Athenaeum* review of Middleton Murry's *Cinnamon and Angelica: A Play*, Eliot writes about poetic drama in a contemporary context: 'The composition of a poetic drama is in fact the most difficult, the most exhausting task that a poet can set himself.'

4 June: Pound writes to Quinn that it is 'a crime against literature' that Eliot should continue to work in Lloyds Bank; and suggests that a subscription be raised to give Eliot an independent income.

10 June: Writing to his wife, Conrad Aiken describes lunches that he has with Eliot in the City: 'Our discussions are grave, tinged here and there with just a glint of guarded humor.'

14 July: Eliot writes to Lytton Strachey declining a weekend invitation because of pressure of work. (Holroyd, 1967).

1 August. Aldous Huxley notes in a letter that a weekend party at Garsington includes the Eliots, as well as the Morrells, Huxley himself and Mark Gertler. The Eliots become regular visitors and in Vivienne's diary in 1935 she mentions: 'How often Ottoline used to say to me — and *how sadly* — "isn't Tom beautiful, Vivienne, such a *fine mind*, such a grand impression. Such a good *walk*." ' (Gordon, 1977).

9 August: Eliot completes his collection of essays, *The Sacred Wood*. He leaves shortly afterwards, with Wyndham Lewis, for a holiday in France; travelling first to Brittany, then to Paris. In *Blasting and Bombardiering* (1937) Wyndham Lewis recounts how Pound gave Eliot a parcel to deliver to James Joyce, living in Paris at this time. Eliot sends Joyce a telegram, inviting him to collect the parcel and have dinner with him and Lewis. In due course Joyce arrives with his son. After much preamble: 'James Joyce was by now attempting to untie the crafty housewifely knots of the cunning old Ezra. . .a fairly presentable pair of *old brown shoes* stood revealed, in the centre of the bourgeois French table.'

Autumn: The mystic P. D. Ouspensky visits London and holds a series of séances, financed by Lady Rothermere. Those occasionally present include Eliot, Herbert Read, and David Garnett, the novelist. (Carswell, 1978).

September: Eliot stays with Leonard and Virginia Woolf at Monk's House, Rodmell, Sussex. Leonard Woolf notes in *Downhill All the Way* (1967): 'In the years 1920 to 1923 Tom Eliot stayed with us several times in Rodmell and he used to come and dine with us at Richmond.'

12 September: Pound writes to the American poet, William Carlos Williams, on the subject of 'kawnscious or unkawnscious': 'Eliot is perfectly conscious of having imitated Laforgue, has worked to get away from it.'

November: In his first article for *The Dial*, Eliot writes on 'The Possibility of a Poetic Drama': 'Possibly the majority of attempts to confect a poetic drama have begun at the wrong end; they have aimed at the small public which wants "poetry".'

4 November: *The Sacred Wood* is published by Methuen, with a dedication to H. W. E. (Henry Ware Eliot, Eliot's father). Most of the essays in it are drawn from reviews of the two previous years. Reviews are generally disappointing; but in spite of this *The Sacred Wood* establishes Eliot as a critic of definite and influential taste. F. W. Bateson, an Oxford undergraduate at this time, later writes: 'Until the publication of *The Waste Land* we were hardly aware of Eliot the poet, whereas we were very much aware of Eliot the critic. *The Sacred Wood* was almost our sacred book.' (Bergonzi, 1972).

2 December: *The Sacred Wood* is reviewed in *The Times Literary Supplement*. The reviewer notes: 'His (Eliot's) criticism is always worth reading and often of great value'; but mentions a 'certain perversity', even a 'malice' against writers such as Meredith and Swinburne, and finds Eliot's opinions sometimes 'capricious'.

Late 1920:   Pound leaves London for Paris, increasingly disillusioned with English intellectual life. Richard Aldington, in *Life for Life's Sake* (1941) compares Pound's achievements in London with those of Eliot: 'by merit, tact, prudence and pertinacity he (Eliot) succeeded in doing what no other American has ever done — imposing his personality, taste, and even many of his opinions on literary England.' In the course of the year, the critic I. A. Richards meets Eliot. Richards later describes (Tate, 1967) visiting him at Lloyds Bank:

> What they showed me was a figure stooping, very like a dark bird in a feeder, over a big table covered with all sorts and sizes of foreign correspondence. The big table almost entirely filled a little room under the street. Within a foot of our heads when we stood were the thick, green glass squares of the pavement on which hammered all but incessantly the heels of the passers-by. There was just room for two perches beside the table . . .

1921

1921-early 1922: Eliot writes several 'London Letters' for *The Dial*; and also reviews books in *Tyro*, Wyndham Lewis's new magazine for the visual arts; *The Chapbook*, Harold Munro's successor to *Poetry and Drama*; and *The Times Literary Supplement*.

March-April: Vivienne Eliot's health breaks down after the illness of her father the previous year.

31 March: On the tercentenary of the birth of Andrew Marvell, the seventeenth-century Puritan poet, Eliot, in an article in *The Times Literary Supplement*, quotes Marvell's poem 'To his Coy Mistress' at length, pointing out its 'alliance of levity and seriousness', also found in Gautier, Ben Jonson, and 'in the *dandyisme* of Baudelaire and Laforgue'; and pleading that Marvell's quality of wit should preserve his reputation.

April: Vivienne Eliot goes to convalesce in the country; Eliot's mother, sister and brother arrive from the USA on a visit. Eliot goes with his brother Henry to see Stravinsky's ballet, *Sacré du printemps*, brought to London by Diaghilev's Ballets Russes; at the end Eliot stands up and cheers.

A poem by Eliot 'Song to the Opherian', signed with the pseudonym Gus Krutzsch, appears in the spring issue of *Tyro*; seven of its thirteen lines are, to appear later, slightly revised, in Eliot's poem 'The wind sprang up at four o'clock'.

In the first of his 'London Letters' for *The Dial*, Eliot writes about music-hall artistes, including Marie Lloyd and Little Tich, currently appearing at the London Palladium. Eliot's enthusiasm for music hall art is also demonstrated in his obituary of Marie Lloyd in *The Criterion* of January 1923; and in *The Use of Poetry and the Use of Criticism* (1933) he will remark upon the similarities between the poet and the music-hall comedian.

9 May: In a letter to Quinn, Eliot mentions that the long poem which becomes 'The Waste Land' is 'partly on paper'. (Valerie Eliot, 1971).

June: In his 'London Letter' in *The Dial*, Eliot deplores the threatened demolition of two historic churches in the City of London, St Mary Woolnoth and St Magnus Martyr. These churches are referred to in line 264 of

'The Fire Sermon' and line 67 of 'The Burial of the Dead' in 'The Waste Land'.

9 June: In a front-page article on Dryden in *The Times Literary Supplement*, Eliot expounds the merits of a poet whom he feels has been too long neglected: 'To those whose taste in poetry is formed entirely upon the English poetry of the nineteenth century – to the majority – it is difficult to explain or excuse Dryden'. Eliot hopes that Dryden's work will be reappraised 'when taste is becoming more fluid and ready for a new mould'.

23 June: Eliot writes to Richard Aldington of his family's visit: 'These new and yet old relationships involve immense tact and innumerable adjustments.' (Valerie Eliot, 1971).

29 June: Lytton Strachey writes to Carrington about a dinner and poetry-reading at the Sitwells at which Eliot appeared, 'very sad and seedy'. (Holroyd, 1967).

August: Writing in *The Dial* in 'London Letter', Eliot remarks: 'Cubism is not licence, but an attempt to establish order.'

16 August: Eliot writes to Richard Aldington, now living in Paris, about his possible involvement with a new literary magazine (to become *The Criterion*). (Valerie Eliot, 1971).

September: Eliot's health having been deteriorating for several months, Vivienne arranges for him to see a specialist, who tells him that he needs three months' complete rest, as soon as possible.

12 October: Eliot goes to Margate, accompanied by Vivienne, who stays with him for the first few days.

20 October: Eliot's review of *Metaphysical Lyrics and Poems of the Seventeenth Century* appears in *The Times Literary Supplement*. The state of mind he describes seems to relate to his own experience in writing 'The Waste Land' at this time:

> When a poet's mind is perfectly equipped for its work, it is constantly amalgamating disparate experience; the ordinary man's experience is chaotic, irregular, fragmentary. The latter falls in love or reads Spinoza, and these two experiences have nothing to do with each other, or with the noise of the typewriter or the smell of cooking; in the mind of the poet these experiences are always forming new wholes.

22 October: Eliot moves to the Albermarle Hotel, Cliftonville, Margate. The 'Fire Sermon' section of 'The Waste Land' is almost certainly written during this time.

End of October: Following a letter from Julian Huxley endorsing Lady Ottoline Morrell's recommendation of a Dr Roger Vittoz in Lausanne, Eliot decides to go to Switzerland for treatment.

12 November: Eliot leaves Margate and returns to London for a week.

18 November: Eliot leaves London for Lausanne. Vivienne accompanies him as far as Paris, where she stays with the Pounds.

Early December.   At a sanatorium at Chardonne, above Vevey, Eliot composes most of the 1000 or so lines which make up the original version of 'The Waste Land'. In 1932, Eliot will recall this period in the series of lectures to become *The Use of Poetry and the Use of Criticism* (1933).

Mid-December: Eliot returns to London via Paris, to show Pound the manuscript of 'The Waste Land'. Pound condemns its length and collaborates with Eliot in deleting eight major sections and making numerous minor alterations, reducing the poem to its final 433 lines. In his article, 'Ezra Pound', in the *New English Weekly*, October 1946, Eliot will pay tribute to Pound's 'editorial genius'.

24 December: Pound writes to Eliot saying that the manuscript is 'MUCH improved'; urging him to keep to the deletions they have made: 'The thing now runs from 'April . . . ' to 'shantih' without a break. That is 19 pages, and let us say the longest poem in the English langwidge. Don't try to bust all records by prolonging it further.' Pound adds a humourous poem, 'Sage Homme', as postscript; describing himself as the midwife of 'The Waste Land'.

1922

January: Eliot answers Pound's letter about 'The Waste Land' manuscript, suggesting further minor alterations. He also asks Pound if he advises printing 'Gerontion' as a prelude; suggests omitting the 'Phlebas' section; suggests including Pound's poem 'Sage Homme' as an epigram; agrees to omit miscellaneous pieces; and queries Pound's suggestion that he should omit a short passage by Joseph Conrad which originally appeared at the beginning of the manuscript. (Paige, 1951).

Late January: Pound replies to Eliot's letter. He agrees to the minor alterations; advises against printing 'Gerontion' as a preface but vehemently argues for retaining the 'Phlebas' section, which is 'an integral part of the poem'. He tells Eliot to do as he thinks fit about his own poem and the Conrad quotation (Eliot omits both).

12 February: Pound writes to John Quinn that Eliot returned from Switzerland with 'a damn good poem'.

March: Pound revives his earlier scheme to raise a private income for Eliot, to release him from Lloyds Bank and allow him to devote himself to his own writing. The plan is called *Bel Esprit* and Pound will attempt to find 30 guarantors of £10 a year for an indefinite period. The scheme is parodied by Lytton Strachey in a letter to the Woolfs in December. (Holroyd, 1967); and eventually peters out, due to a lack of committed contributors (although Quinn promises $300 for five years) and the attitude of Eliot himself, evident in his letter of 30 June to Richard Aldington.

June. Virginia Woolf writes in her *Diary* that Eliot comes to Hogarth House to read a new poem of 'great beauty and force of phrase; symmetry and tensity'.

7 June: Conrad Aiken writes to Maurice Firuski: ' "Literary people are shits", gravely observed Eliot to me at lunch this winter; he said a mouthful. I recognized myself instantly.'

25 June: Eliot writes to Quinn about his 'long poem', saying that the American publishers Liveright have made him an offer of it; and asking Quinn to clarify the contract. He says of the poem: 'I think it is the best I have ever done, and Pound thinks so too.' (Valerie Eliot, 1971).

30 June: Eliot writes to Richard Aldington that he appreciates the motives of Pound in trying to set up a fund for him, but feels it verges on 'precarious and slightly undignified charity'. (Valerie Eliot, 1971).

7 September: Gilbert Seddes, the managing editor of *The Dial*, meets Liveright in Quinn's office in New York, as *The Dial* are anxious to be the first to publish 'The Waste Land'. It is agreed that Eliot will receive *The Dial*'s annual award of $2000, and that *The Dial* will publish the poem first, without notes, and buy 350 copies of the book.

21 September: Eliot writes to Quinn, thanking him for all his efforts on his behalf and saying that he feels Pound deserves *The Dial*'s award more than he does. He also says that he is sending Quinn the original manuscript of 'The Waste Land', which he feels is worth preserving as evidence of Pound's contribution. This manuscript is subsequently mislaid and not traced until 1968; it will be published in 1971 as *T. S. Eliot: The Waste Land, a facsimile & transcript*, edited by Valerie Eliot.

October: The first issue of the quarterly edited by Eliot, *The Criterion*, is published. Eliot found the backer through his friend, Richard Cobden Sanderson, the private publisher, who introduced him to Lady Rothermere, wife of the first Viscount Rothermere, the press baron. For three years Lady Rothermere, interested in painting and literature, is sole owner of *The Criterion* and subsidizes it generously.

The first issue of *The Criterion* contains 'The Waste Land' (its first publication in any form), and six other contributions, among which are a translation of Dostoevsky's 'Plan of a Novel', by S. S. Koteliansky and Virginia Woolf, 'German Poetry of Today', by Hermann Hesse, and an article on Joyce's *Ulysses* by Valéry Larbaud, published with an acknowledgement to the *Nouvelle Revue Française*. *The Criterion* becomes one of Eliot's mouthpieces, and his way of presenting to an (albeit small) readership the most important names and trends in English and European literature; though he continues to write reviews for other periodicals and newspapers.

November: 'The Waste Land' has its first American publication, in *The Dial*. In tribute to Pound's work on the manuscript, Eliot dedicates the poem to him, *'il miglior fabbro'* (a quotation from Dante — 'the better craftsman').

15 December: *The Waste Land* appears in book form, published by Boni & Liveright of New York. For this edition notes are added, which also appear in all subsequent editions. In *The Frontiers of Criticism* (1956) Eliot will describe how the notes were added simply because the book was too short; though on 10 September 1924 Arnold Bennett will describe how Eliot told him the notes were 'serious'.

Richard Aldington, who later becomes jealous of Eliot's success, writes in *Stepping Heavenward* (1931) a malicious fictionalization of Eliot at about this time. Eliot is parodied as 'Cibber'.

"America must really be a *wonderful* country," she continued.
"Ye—es." replied Cibber thoughtfully. "Ye—es, but it has many defects. It is essentially a country with too many moralities and too few manners. It can only be rescued by a disciplined aristocracy and a dogmatic Church."

1923

January: The second issue of *The Criterion* appears, its contents including an obituary by Eliot on Marie Lloyd, the music hall artiste; 'The Shrine', a short story by Luigi Pirandello; and Roger Fry's translation of Mallarmé's poem, 'Hérodiade'.

7 February: A review of *The Waste Land* by Conrad Aiken appears in the journal *The New Republic*, subtitled 'An Anatomy of Melancholy'. Aiken later (Tate, 1967) remarks: 'I suspect it was the first full-length favorable review the poem had then received.'

23 February: In a letter to Lytton Strachey, Virginia Woolf mentions that Eliot has been offered the post of literary editor of *The Nation*.

26 February: Quinn acknowledges the manuscript that Eliot has sent him, and insists on paying him $140 for it. He comments that, in Eliot's place, he would not have followed all Pound's suggestions. (Valerie Eliot, 1971).

4 March: Vivienne Eliot writes to Mary Hutchinson that she would be unwilling for Eliot to leave Lloyds Bank, as she feels it would prejudice their financial position. (Gordon, 1977).

12 March: Eliot writes to Quinn thanking him for payment of the manuscript of 'The Waste Land'; and mentioning his exhaustion, caused by the extra work that editing *The Criterion* entails. (Valerie Eliot, 1971).

15 March: Quinn writes to Eliot that he has sent Eliot's books to various people who might become guarantors, that so far only Otto Kahn, the international banker, has responded; and that he hopes to be able to raise at least $1000 for Eliot. (Valerie Eliot, 1971).

27 March: Quinn cables to Eliot that, if Eliot accepts *The Nation's* offer of the post of literary editor (see 23 February) he will receive $600 annually for five years – $400 from Quinn himself and $200 from Otto Khan. He also advises Eliot that *The Nation* should guarantee him one year's pay. (Valerie Eliot, 1971).

April: The April issue of *The Criterion* (number three) includes 'A Preface' (to *La Croix des Roses*) by Julien Benda, a French philosopher with whom Eliot felt many affinities; 'In the Orchard' by Virginia Woolf; translations of two of Dostoevsky's letters; 'The Nature of Metaphysical Poetry', an article by Herbert Read; and a translation of 'The Serpent' by Paul Valéry. In 'Dramatis Personae', Eliot notes the death of Sarah Bernhardt, the French actress, and in a discussion of drama as ritual comments: 'the failure of the contemporary stage to satisfy the craving for ritual is one of the reasons why it is not a living art.'

Early April: Vivienne has an acute colitis attack and nearly dies. Eliot takes his three weeks' annual holiday from the bank to instal her in a cottage near Chichester.

2 April: Eliot cables to Quinn that, *The Nation* having failed to guarantee him a year's pay, he has rejected their offer. (The post is accepted by Leonard Woolf). He asks Quinn if his offer will still apply if ill-health makes him leave the bank without other employment in view. Quinn cables back that the offer is unconditional and for a period of five years. (Valerie Eliot, 1971).

26 April: Eliot writes to Quinn from Chichester telling him of Vivienne's ill health, and that this is the main cause of his need for financial security. He asks Quinn if the guarantee of $600 will apply if he leaves the bank for another job, or, reiterating his question in the cable of 2 April, if he is forced to leave because of ill health. Eliot also states his intention of leaving the bank. (Valerie Eliot, 1971).

9 June: Eliot writes his first review for the newly combined *The Nation & Athenaeum* (on *The Love Poems of John Donne*).

July: *The Criterion* (number four) contains 'A Biographical Fragment' by W. B. Yeats; 'Notes on a Possible Generalisation of the Theories of Freud' by Jacques Rivière; 'The Malatesta Cantos' by Ezra Pound; 'Pan', a humourous piece on the betel-leaf, by E. M. Forster; and, for the first time, reviews of French, German and American literary periodicals. In a pamphlet inserted to announce the second volume for the autumn, Eliot defines the aims of *The Criterion*: 'The CRITERION aims at the examination of first principles in criticism, at the valuation of new, and the re-valuation of old works of literature according to principles, and the illustration of these principles in creative writing.'

23 July: In a letter to Eliot, Quinn encloses a draft for £86.19s.1d (the equivalent of $400), Otto Kahn's offer having proved to be conditional on Eliot's leaving the bank. Quinn tells Eliot that he can rely on the same sum annually for the next four years.

12 September: The first British edition of *The Waste Land* is published by the Woolfs at the Hogarth Press. As with *The Sacred Wood*, its reception by the literary establishment is cool though not disrespectful. *The Times Literary Supplement* talks of a 'disinclination to awake in us a direct emotional response' and feels that 'some unsympathetic tug has set Mr. Eliot's gift awry'. However, the poem is cumulatively recognised as a piece of outstanding modern poetry; and Edmund Wilson writes in *Axel's Castle* (1931): 'Where some of even the finest intelligences of the elder generation read *The Waste Land* with blankness or laughter, the young had recognised a poet.' E. M. Forster later comments (1928) on Eliot's popularity with younger readers: 'Mr Eliot's work, particularly *The Waste Land*, has made a profound impression on them, and given them precisely the food they needed . . . He is the most important author of their day.' From the first the poem arouses much critical debate, and Eliot later will comment on its reception in *Thoughts after Lambeth* (1931).

4 October: Eliot writes to Quinn that he will consider the money sent to him as a kind of emergency fund. He describes all the financial difficulties of Vivienne's illness and expresses his thanks to Quinn in the strongest terms. (Valerie Eliot, 1971).

15 October: Eliot writes to Bertrand Russell in answer to a letter that Russell has written congratulating Eliot on 'The Waste Land'. Eliot is particularly gratified that Russell likes Part V: 'the only part that justifies the whole, at all'. (Russell, 1967).

November: Wyndham Lewis writes to Eliot, saying that he will contribute to *The Criterion* for nothing, as Eliot did to *Blast*. Lewis says that the failure of 'an exceptional attempt like yours with *The Criterion*' would mean that 'the chance of establishing some sort of critical standard here is diminished.'

Eliot writes a review of Joyce's *Ulysses* in *The Dial*: 'In using the myth, in manipulating a continuous parallel between contemporaneity and antiquity, Mr. Joyce is pursuing a method which others must pursue after him.'

10 December: Eliot writes to Lytton Strachey asking him for a contribution to *The Criterion*, and suggesting Macaulay as a subject. (Holroyd, 1967). A piece by Strachey on Macaulay will be published in *The Nation & Athenaeum* in 1928.

At some time during 1923 Eliot is introduced by Richard Cobden-Sanderson to William Force Stead, an ex-diplomat who has taken holy orders. Stead draws Eliot towards the writings of seventeenth century Anglicans, especially those of Lancelot Andrewes; encouraging the spiritual progression which leads Eliot towards baptism into the Church of England.

1924

February: *The Criterion* includes the essay, 'Four Elizabethan Dramatists' by Eliot; a fragment of a novel by Wyndham Lewis; and 'Notes on Art and Life' by Gerhart Hauptmann. The foreign reviews look at German, Dutch, Danish, Italian and American periodicals. It also contains 'Letters of the Moment', signed 'F.M.', a pseudonym for Vivienne Eliot; under the names of Fanny Marlow, Feiron Morris and Felix Morrison, she becomes a regular contributor until July 1925.

Spring: Vivienne is acutely ill of what is unsatisfactorily diagnosed as rheumatism.

April: For the first time *The Criterion* contains an editorial 'Commentary' by Eliot, later to become a regular feature. In this 'Commentary' Eliot writes about a posthumous work, *Speculations* by T. E. Hulme (who had been one of Pound's circle before being killed in World War I): 'Hulme is classical, reactionary and revolutionary; he is the antipodes of the eclectic, tolerant and democratic mind of the end of the last century.' Eliot also discusses an article by Bertrand Russell which appeared in the March issue of *The Dial*, in which Russell describes the nineteenth century as a period of distinction for its scientists rather than its philosophers, artists or literary men. Eliot deplores such opinions from the author of *The Philosophy of Leibnitz* (1900) and *Principia Mathematica* (1910); both books that Eliot admires. This issue also contains 'On the Style of Marcel Proust', by E. R. Curtius; an article by Ezra Pound on the modern American musician George Antheil; and 'Letters of the Moment II' by 'F.M.' (Vivienne Eliot), which includes 20 lines of verse by Eliot from the 'Fresca' section of the original *Waste Land* manuscript (edited out by Pound).

July: The July issue of *The Criterion* includes 'The Death of Albertine' by Proust (translated by C. K. Scott Moncrieff); 'The Cat and the Moon' by W. B. Yeats; 'Character in Fiction' a reprinted paper by Virginia Woolf; 'Ithaca', a poem by C. P. Cavafy (the greatest of modern Greek poets); 'Art Chronicle' by Wyndham Lewis (to become a regular feature); 'Books of the Quarter', *The Criterion*'s first book reviews, in which 'F.M.' (Vivienne Eliot) reviews novels by David Garnett and Middleton Murry. Eliot himself reviews *The Growth of Civilisation and The Origin of Magic and Religion*, wondering whether it is possible for art to survive divorced from its original, primitive functions; he also notes the closure of the Egoist Press, praising it for having made possible the publication of works that would not have been accepted by larger publishing houses.

28 July: John Quinn dies at the age of 54.

10 September: Arnold Bennett notes in his *Journals* that he met Eliot at the Reform Club, and that Eliot told him about his work at Lloyds Bank: 'Interesting work, he said, but he would prefer to be doing something else.'

He also notes: 'He (Eliot) wanted to write a drama of modern life (furnished flat sort of people) in a rhythmic prose "perhaps with certain things in it accentuated by drum-beats". And he wanted my advice. We arranged that he should do the scenario and some sample pages of dialogue.'

October: The October issue of *The Criterion* includes 'Jimmy and the Desperate Woman', a short story by D. H. Lawrence; and a 'Commentary' in which Eliot pays tribute to the recently deceased F. H. Bradley (on whose book *Knowledge and Experience* Eliot had written his doctoral thesis). He criticizes Shaw's *St Joan*, currently in its first production, commenting that Shaw has committed a sacrilege in making her: 'a great middle-class reformer' whose place is 'a little higher than Mrs. Pankhurst'. The issue also includes 'Art Chronicle', in which Wyndham Lewis reviews a folio of contemporary artists printed for *The Dial*, among whom are Picasso, Vlaminck and Matisse; a new section, 'Music', in which J. B. Trend comments adversely on the British National Opera Company, and praises the Salzburg festival, then in its third year; 'Foreign Theatre' which describes a seven-week modern ballet and drama festival in Paris; 'Books of the Quarter' which includes Herbert Read reviewing *Democracy and Leadership* by Irving Babbitt (whose courses Eliot had attended at Harvard), and I. P. Fassett reviewing E. M. Forster's *A Passage to India.*

30 October: *Homage to John Dryden: Three Essays on Poetry in the 17th Century* is published by the Hogarth Press as part of the Hogarth Essays Series, from essays which first appeared in *The Times Literary Supplement* in 1921. In book form, these essays are 'incalculably influential' (Bergonzi, 1972), leading to a reappraisal, even rediscovery, of their subjects; and confirming, with *The Sacred Wood*, Eliot's importance as a critic. F. R. Leavis later writes (*Anna Karenina and Other Essays*, 1967): 'It was the impact of this slender new collection that sent one back to *The Sacred Wood* and confirmed with decisive practical effect one's sense of the stimulus to be got from that rare thing, a fine intelligence in literary criticism.'

In a letter to Herbert Read about *The Criterion* (Tate, 1967) Eliot discusses the fact that a 'dogma' is needed for the periodical, but adds that he does not expect his readers to share his religious or intellectual opinions.

Winter: The French magazine *Commerce* prints 'Poème' by Eliot, in an English text with a French translation; reprinted as Part I of 'The Hollow Men'.

During the winter of 1924—25 Vivienne Eliot suffers another illness which is nearly fatal.

November: The *Chapbook* publishes three poems by Eliot under the heading 'Doris's Dream Songs': 'Eyes that last I saw in tears', 'The wind sprang up at four o'clock', and 'This is the dead land'. (The latter becomes Part III of 'The Hollow Men').

December: A translation of Paul Valéry's *Le Serpent* is published for *The Criterion* by Richard Cobden-Sanderson, with an introduction by Eliot.

1925

January: The January issue of *The Criterion* contains 'Three Poems' by Eliot – 'Eyes I dare not meet in dreams', 'Eyes that last I saw in tears', and 'The eyes are not here'; the last two to be included in 'The Hollow Men'. This issue also includes 'On the Eve', a 'dialogue' purportedly written by Eliot but actually written by Vivienne; 'A Diary of the Rive Gauche' by 'F.M.' (Vivienne); and reviews of ten books, the titles listed on the front cover for the first time.

31 January: Eliot writes to Wyndham Lewis, requesting a more substantial contribution to *The Criterion* than in previous issues, and assuring him that, because of his financial difficulties, he would receive better terms of payment than other contributors. Eliot mentions that he himself receives no salary for editing *The Criterion*. (Rose, 1963).

March: Eliot's 'The Hollow Men' is published in *The Dial* – an early version that omits Part III.

April: *The Criterion* includes a short story, 'The Field of Mustard', by A. E. Coppard; 'On the Nature of Allegory', an essay by Benedetto Croce; a poem, 'Necesse est Perstare', by 'F.M.' (Vivienne Eliot); and a sketch, 'Night Club', by Feiron Morris (Vivienne Eliot). Eliot himself reviews two books about dancing, but the 'Commentary' refers to 'Mr. T.S.E.'s severe illness'.

7 May: Eliot writes to Bertrand Russell describing Vivienne's deteriorating health, and praising her writing ability: 'She writes *extremely* well (stories, etc.) and with great originality.' (Russell, 1967).

July: *The Criterion* includes 'Notes on Language and Style' by T. E. Hulme, edited by Herbert Read; 'Fragment of an Unpublished Work' by James Joyce; 'The Woman Who Rode Away', by D. H. Lawrence; and 'Fete Galante' by Fanny Marlow (Vivienne; her last contribution to *The Criterion*, purportedly a fictional sketch but containing a thinly veiled portrait of herself and Eliot who appears, in an unflattering description, as 'the American financier' and also as 'a poet'). An editorial note states that Miss Fanny Marlow is unable to continue her 'Diary of the Rive Gauche' owing to illness.

The Criterion now ceases publication until January 1926, as during this month Lady Rothermere's original contract expires, and she is unwilling to continue to be *The Criterion*'s sole financial backer. Through the friendship of Bruce Richmond, the editor of *The Times Literary Supplement*, with Frank Morley, who works in the recently formed publishing house of Faber & Gwyer, it is agreed that the cost of *The New Criterion* will be divided between Faber & Gwyer and Lady Rothermere, with Eliot remaining sole editor.

November: Eliot leaves Lloyds Bank to become a director of Faber &

Gwyer. He has been recommended to Geoffrey Faber by Bruce Richmond, editor of *The Times Literary Supplement*, Frank Morley, an American co-director, and Hugh Walpole, the novelist; Frank Morley later recalls (Tate, 1967) that Eliot was originally taken on, not as a literary adviser, but as a 'man of business'. Eliot will later recall (in his tribute to Geoffrey Faber, *The Times* 1 April 1962) that: 'both the original directors and new members were inexperienced in general publishing'.

At Faber & Gwyer (renamed Faber & Faber in March 1929) Eliot carries out the usual administrative duties of a director, but becomes increasingly occupied with editorial work; eventually becoming responsible for the Faber poetry list, which will introduce to the public a new generation of British poets.

23 November: *Poems 1909–1925* is published by Faber & Gwyer.

17 December: Eliot writes to Leonard Woolf that he wishes to close an unhappy period of his life and make a new beginning. (Gordon, 1977).

30 December: Conrad Aiken remarks, in a letter to Maurice Firuski, that Eliot's *Poems 1909–1925* has already sold 700 copies.

1926

January: *The New Criterion* (called by this title until January 1927) includes a general statement, 'The Idea of a Literary Review', by Eliot; 'On Being Ill', by Virginia Woolf; 'The Monocle', by Aldous Huxley; and 'The Woman Who Rode Away – II', a short story by D. H. Lawrence.

4 January: In a letter to Robert Linscott, Conrad Aiken recounts how he wrote from hospital to Eliot, congratulating him on *Poems 1909–1925*; and how Eliot replied by sending him a page from the *Midwives Gazette*, with the words 'purulent offensive discharge', amongst others, underlined.

March: *Savanarola*, a long dramatic poem by Eliot's mother, Charlotte Champe Eliot, is published by Richard Cobden-Sanderson, in an edition of 300 copies, with an introduction by Eliot.

4 March: Anonymously reviewing the *Oxford Book of English Prose* in *The Times Literary Supplement*, Eliot compares a selected passage from Lytton Strachey's *Queen Victoria* with a passage from Joyce's *Ulysses*, not in the anthology; illustrating Joyce's superiority as an innovator of language and style.

April: *The New Criterion* includes an article on 'The Novels of Virginia Woolf', by E. M. Forster; and 'Our Need for Religious Sincerity', by W. B. Yeats.

June: *The New Criterion* includes 'Mornings in Mexico' by D. H. Lawrence; and 'The Romantic Fallacy' by J. Middleton Murry. In his 'Commentary' Eliot discusses Sunday theatrical societies and the possible founding of a National Theatre. He himself would have no confidence in such a scheme, as he feels there would inevitably be shortcomings in any administrators.

23 September: An unsigned article by Eliot on 'Lancelot Andrewes' appears in *The Times Literary Supplement*. In this article – the first to indicate that Eliot is increasingly attracted by Anglican forms of worship – he states that Andrewes, who was Bishop of Chichester, Ely and Winchester between 1605 and 1626, and the most celebrated preacher of his day, is 'the first great preacher of the English Catholic Church'. As an example of Andrewes' prose, Eliot cites a passage which will be remoulded by him in his poem 'The Journey of the Magi' (1927):

> It was no summer progress. A cold coming they had of it at this time of the year, just the worst time of the year to take a journey, and specially a long journey in. The way so deep, the weather sharp, the days short, the sun farthest off, *in solstitio brumae*, 'the very dead of winter'.

October: *The New Criterion* includes 'The Lament of Saint Denis', a poem by Herbert Read; and 'Fragment of a Prologue' by Eliot, his first printed piece of dramatic poetry.

1927

January: *The New Criterion* contains Eliot's 'Fragment of an Agon'. (*The New Criterion* briefly ceases publication until its reappearence as a monthly in May.)

Eliot's 'Note on Poetry and Belief' is published in the first number of Wyndham Lewis' new magazine, *The Enemy*: 'I cannot see that poetry can ever be separated from something which I should call belief.'

18 March: Eliot gives an address, 'Shakespeare and the Stoicism of Seneca', to the Shakespeare Association; it will be published in September. Eliot discusses the influence of Seneca on Shakespeare's tragic heroes; particularly evident in 'the attitude of self-dramatization assumed . . . at moments of tragic intensity'.

May: *The Monthly Criterion* is published, and appears every month until March 1928; from June 1928 to its demise in January 1939 it reverts to being a quarterly. *The Monthly Criterion* is shorter than the quarterly, with fewer articles, but deals with the same topics and uses many of the same contributors as those of the previous five years.

5 May: An article on Baudelaire by Eliot is printed in *The Dial*. Eliot stresses the more Christian aspects of Baudelaire and how he acquired 'the most difficult, of the Christian virtues, the virtue of humility'.

June: Vivienne's health again having deteriorated, Eliot goes with her to a centre for nervous disorders at Divonne-les-Bains, near Geneva. At the centre undergoing treatment at the same time is Robert Sencourt, specialist on Dante and prominent Anglican, and he later recalls Vivienne's appearance: 'Her black hair was dank, her white face blotched — owing, no doubt, to the excess of bromide she had been taking. Her dark dress hung loosely over her frail form; her expression was both vague and acutely sad.' (Sencourt, 1971).

Sencourt gives Eliot an introduction to Lord Halifax, the leading layman in the Church of England and a spokesman for Catholic unity, and Eliot stays with him at Hickleton Hall near Doncaster on his return to England.

16 June: Eliot's article on Machiavelli is printed in *The Times Literary Supplement*. Eliot defends Machiavelli against the usual change of being a cynic, maintaining that Machiavelli showed how 'the neglect of religion. . . had contributed to the ruin of Italy', and that Machiavelli is 'a man who accepted in his own fashion the orthodox view of original sin'.

29 June: Eliot is baptized into the Church of England by William Force Stead, in Finstock church, Oxfordshire. (Eliot is regarded as unbaptized, as Unitarians reject the formula 'in the Name of the Father, and of the Son and of the Holy Ghost'). Eliot's godfathers are two friends of Stead's: the theologian B. H. Streeter, later Provost of Queen's College, Oxford, and Vere Somerset, historian and fellow of Worcester College, Oxford.

30 June: Eliot is confirmed in the Church of England at Cuddesdon, the theological college near Oxford, by Thomas Banks Strong, Bishop of Oxford.

July: An article by Eliot, 'Archbishop Bramhall', on the Bishop of Derry under Charles I and Primate of Ireland under Charles II, is printed in *Theology*. Eliot gives an account of Bramhall's reform of the Irish Church and how he tried to 'bring it into conformity with the English Church'.

25 August: Eliot's poem, 'The Journey of the Magi', is published by Faber & Faber, with drawings by E. McKnight Kauffer. The content of the poem is generally agreed to reflect Eliot's state of mind in transition between his old and new faiths. 'Journey of the Magi' is the first in a series of poems Eliot later groups together as the 'Ariel Poems'; and in an interview with *The New York Times Book Review*, 29 November 1953, he will describe how, after 'The Hollow Men', he thought he had no more poetry in him, but that writing the 'Ariel Poems' 'released the stream' and led directly to 'Ash Wednesday'. The Other 'Ariel Poems' are 'A Song for Simeon', 'Animula', 'Marina', and 'The Cultivation of Christmas Trees'.

September: *Seneca His Tenne Tragedies* — Elizabethan translations of the Roman dramatist — is published by Constable and Co. with an introduction by Eliot, in which he shows himself especially interested in the quality of the verse, which he believes was not intended to be performed but was for recitation only. This principle reappears in Eliot's use of the chorus in his own plays.

2 November: Eliot becomes a naturalized British citizen.

10 December: A poem by Eliot, 'Salutation', is published in the *Saturday Review of Literature*.

During 1927, Eliot contributes to the *Nouvelle Revue Francaise, The Nation & Athenaeum, The Dial, Theology*, and *The Times Literary Supplement*.

1928

January: *The Monthly Criterion* contains Eliot's poem 'Salutation'; also 'Prologue to an Essay on Criticism', by Charles Maurras, translated by Eliot. In this and subsequent issues Eliot defends Maurras against charges made by Leo Ward, a Roman Catholic pamphleteer, that Maurras has anti-Christian tendencies. Eliot states that Maurras had 'the opposite effect' on him.

March: Eliot makes confession for the first time, to his spiritual director, Father Underhill, later Dean of Rochester and then Bishop of Bath and Wells. (Gordon, 1977).

Spring: The French magazine *Commerce* publishes Eliot's poem, 'Perch'io non spero', in English text with French translation; this becomes Part I of 'Ash Wednesday'.

23 April: Eliot writes to Herbert Read about the lack of national identity that he has always felt. (Tate, 1967).

May: *Of Dramatick Poesie: An Essay, 1668* by Dryden is published, with a preface, 'Dialogue on Poetic Drama', by Eliot. In this essay, characters A, B, C, D and E debate the question of verse drama versus prose drama.

June: *The Monthly Criterion* reverts to being a quarterly. In the last issue of *The Criterion* (January 1939) Eliot will comment on this decision.

July: Eliot's article, 'The Humanism of Irving Babbitt' is printed in *Forum*. Writing of Babbitt, whose courses Eliot attended whilst studying for his master's degree at Harvard, Eliot says that he knew that: 'the Christian religion is an essential part of the history of our race'.

17 September: *This American World* by Edgar Mowrer is published with a preface by Eliot. In the preface, Eliot writes about his geographical background:

> The family guarded jealously its connections with New England; but it was not until years of maturity that I perceived that I myself had always been a New Englander in the South West, and a South Westerner in New England. . .In New England I missed the long dark river, the ailanthus trees, the flaming cardinal birds, the high limestone bluffs where we searched for fossil shellfish; in Missouri I missed

the fir trees, the bay and golden rod, the song-sparrows, the red granite and the blue sea of Massachussetts.

24 September: Eliot's poem, *A Song for Simeon*, is published by Faber & Gwyer, with drawings by E. McKnight Kauffer. Simeon, as the old man who just before he dies sees the infant Jesus, symbolizes the man for whom only the first stage of faith is possible.

4 October: *Fishermen of the Banks*, a collection of short stories by James B. Connolly, and a boyhood favourite of Eliot's, is republished by Faber & Gwyer. In his short preface Eliot remembers the town of Gloucester (near which his family had a summer house) and its harbour, and comments: 'The heroes of these narratives are not imaginary heroes, but real.'

20 November: Eliot's collection of essays, *For Lancelot Andrewes: Essays on Style and Order*, is published by Faber & Gwyer. In his preface Eliot states his reason for having chosen the eight essays that make up the book: 'I wished to indicate certain lines of development, and to disassociate myself from certain conclusions which have been drawn from my volume of essays, *The Sacred Wood*.' He continues: 'The general point of view may be described as classicism in literature, royalist in politics, and anglo-catholic in religion.' The eight essays that Eliot has chosen from articles written over the previous two years all place the different subjects in the religious context of their time.

23 November: *Selected Poems* by Ezra Pound is published by Faber & Gwyer, edited and with an introduction by Eliot. Eliot states that the book is intended as an introduction and defends Pound against charges of being antiquarian and uneven in quality, saying that a poet's work can 'proceed along two lines on an imaginary graph', the one an 'effort in technical excellence' and the other his 'normal human course of development', and that only when the two lines 'converge at a high peak . . . do we get a masterpiece'.

December: In his 'Commentary' in *The Criterion*, 'City City', Eliot notes all the current new building in the City, particularly the new banks: 'Those who can remember the city as long ago as 1920 must feel very sad.' In the same issue, in 'The Literature of Fascism', Eliot examines some recent books about Italian fascism; wonders if its example will spread in the rest of Europe; and ascribes fascism to a failure of democracy — not democracy as an idea, but how it is practised. He also comments: 'Most of the concepts which might have attracted me in fascism I seem already to have found, in a more digestible form, in the works of Charles Maurras.'

2 December: *The Times Literary Supplement* reviews *For Lancelot Andrewes: Essays on Style and Order*, paying tribute to Eliot's merits as 'a critical and poetic mind of a high and original order' but reading with 'increasing perturbation' and expressing surprise at the contents of the book: 'From the author of *The Waste Land* it is at first sight astonishing, to say the least.' The reviewer concludes by suggesting that Eliot has rejected 'modernism for mediaevalism'.

Describing Eliot's reputation at this period, James Reeves will write (Marsh and Tambimuttu, 1948), remembering his time as a Cambridge undergraduate:

> Eliot was not at this time 'officially' recognized. . .the more rebellious (lecturers) were enthusiastic, the more conventional loudly and derisively hostile. The 'centre' were temperately and critically sympathetic towards what they recognized as an important new influence, even though it was hailed with undiscriminating adulation by intellectual undergraduates.

1929

March: Faber & Gwyer is renamed Faber & Faber, following the withdrawal of the Gwyer interest. Eliot will pay tribute to Geoffrey Faber (*The Times*, 1 April 1961) for his courage in undertaking sole financial responsibility for the new company.

May: In a letter printed in the last issue of *The Little Review*, Eliot remembers it with gratitude as 'the only periodical which would accept my work, and indeed the only periodical there (the USA) in which I cared to appear'.

12 June: *The Listener* prints 'The Tudor Translators', the first of five talks that Eliot broadcasts during June and July on sixteenth and seventeenth century prose writers. The others are: 'The Elizabethan Grub Street' (19 June), 'The Prose of the Pracher: The Sermons of Donne' (3 July), 'Elizabethan Travellers' Tales' (10 July), and 'The Tudor Biographer' (17 July).

July: *The Criterion* announces an annual short story competition run in conjunction with four other European literary periodicals; the winning story eventually to be translated and published by them in turn. In the last issue of *The Criterion* (January 1939) Eliot will look back on this issue as an embodiment of what he wished to achieve in the way of a literary magazine publishing the best of European thought; also listing some of the foreign writers he had introduced to a British readership – Proust, Valéry and Cocteau amongst others. The winning story of the competition is only translated into one language and the competition is never repeated.

16 July: James Joyce writes to Harriet Weaver from Torquay: 'T.S.E. most friendly. He wants his firm to publish S.G.'s book (Stuart Gilbert's *Study of Ulysses*) and to bring out an English paperback edition of 2/- of A.L.P. (Anna Livia Plurabelle).'

Autumn: *Commerce* publishes Eliot's poem 'Som de L'Escalina' in English text with French translation; reprinted as Part III of 'Ash Wednesday'.

10 September: Charlotte Champe Eliot, Eliot's mother, dies.

27 September: *Dante*, by Eliot, is published by Faber & Faber in their *Poets on Poets* series, and is dedicated to Charles Maurras. Eliot states in a preface that: 'My purpose has been to persuade the reader first of the importance of Dante as a master — I may even say, *the* master, for a poet writing today in any language.'

9 October: Eliot's poem 'Animula' is published by Faber & Faber, with wood engravings by Gertrude Hermes. The poem is a description of the rudimentary, purely physical being, unenlightened by religious faith.

1930

January: Eliot publishes the work of W. H. Auden for the first time in *The Criterion* ('Paid on Both Sides'); Auden's *Poems* is also published by Faber & Faber in 1930.

12 March: *The Listener* publishes 'Thinking in Verse: A Survey of Early Seventeenth Century Poetry' by Eliot, the first of six talks on seventeenth-century writers that Eliot broadcasts during March and April, and which follow chronologically from his broadcasts of June and July 1929. The others are: 'Rhyme and Reason: The Poetry of John Donne' (19 March), 'The Devotional Poets of the 17th century: Donne, Herbert and Crawshaw' (26 March), 'Mystic and Politician as Poet: Vaughan, Traherne, Marvell and Milton' (2 April), 'The Minor Metaphysicals: from Cowley to Dryden' (9 April) and 'John Dryden' (16 April).

24 April: *Ash-Wednesday*, Eliot's first long poem of explicit religious faith, is published by Faber & Faber. It is reviewed with other poems in *Poetry*; the reviewer, typically, is surprised by Eliot's move towards Christian poetry: 'Mr. Eliot's religious experience has not thus far impressed one as conceived in intellectual necessity, or as imposed through other than aesthetic forces on a crowded and exhausted mind.' *Ash-Wednesday* is described as 'a desultory kind of allegory'.

22 May: *Anabasis*, by St John Perse, translated from the French by Eliot, is published by Faber & Faber. In his preface Eliot says that he considers this book as important as Joyce's later work, and defends it (and implicitly, his own poetry) against the charge of obscurity.

25 July: G. Wilson Knight's book on Shakespearian tragedy, *The Wheel of Fire*, is published by Faber & Faber, with an introduction by Eliot in which he commends Knight's preference for interpretation rather than criticism.

9 August: In a letter to William Force Stead, Eliot mentions his own long-cherished intention to explore a mode of writing neglected in the twentieth century – the spiritual autobiography (a possible description of Eliot's last long poem, the *Four Quartets*). (Gordon, 1977).

September: The *Intimate Journals* of Charles Baudelaire, translated by Christopher Isherwood, are published by Blackamore Press, with an introduction by Eliot; who says that Baudelaire would surely have approved of these words of T. E. Hulme: 'Order is thus not merely negative, but creative and liberating. Institutions are necessary.'

25 September: *Marina* is published by Blackamore Press, with drawings by E. McKnight Kauffer. This poem seems to be celebrating the happiness of religious faith, expressed through images of the coast, the sea and sailing.

5 October: A letter from Eliot appears in the *St Louis Post-Dispatch*, under the heading 'From a Distinguished Former St Louisan'. In the letter, Eliot recalls his childhood:

> As I spent the first sixteen years of my life in St Louis, it is evident that St Louis affected me more deeply than any other environment has done. These sixteen years were spent in a house at 2635 Locust Street, since demolished. This house stood on a large piece of land which had belonged to my grandfather, on which there had been negro quarters in his time; in my childhood my grandmother still lived at a house at 2660 Washington Avenue, round the corner. The earliest personal influence I remember, besides that of my parents, was an Irish nursemaid named Annie Dunne, to whom I was greatly attached. . .The river also made a deep impression on me, and it was a great treat to be taken down to the Eads Bridge in flood time.

31 October: Conrad Aiken, in a letter to Theodore Spencer, describes a recent lunch with Eliot, the deterioration of Vivienne's health and of their marriage.

Autumn: *London: A Poem* and *The Vanity of Human Wishes*, Samuel Johnson's satiric poem, is reprinted by Faber & Faber, with an introductory essay by Eliot, in which he states that, after Pope, there are two kinds of eighteenth-century poets worth reading: 'those who, however imperfectly, attempted innovations in idiom, and those who were just conservative enough in sensibility to be able to devise an interesting variation on the old idiom'; Johnson being one of the latter.

Early December: Eliot spends the weekend with George Bell, Bishop of Chichester. Bishop Bell has recently started the Canterbury Festival for religious drama and suggests to Eliot that at some time he might be able to contribute. The meeting is not immediately fruitful, but Eliot is introduced to E. Martin Browne, recently appointed as director of religious drama for the diocese, who is later to direct all his plays.

2 December: Eliot writes to William Force Stead that one of his first tasks as a Christian has been to come to terms with celibacy and to find it easy for the first time. (Gordon, 1977).

During 1930 the Eliots move to no.68 Clarence Gate Gardens, near to an Anglo-Catholic church, St Cyprian's, at which Eliot is a daily worshipper. Francis Underhill continues to be Eliot's spiritual counsellor and introduces

Eliot to Kelham Theological College, near Newark in Nottinghamshire, where he often stays in the 1930s. Eliot becomes an increasingly devout Christian. Robert Sencourt recalls (1971) that, when in 1930 Eliot was invited to lunch by Lady Astor, another American, he refused on grounds that included the fact that she was a divorced woman.

1931

5 March: Eliot's *Thoughts After Lambeth*, in which he comments on a statement issued by the Anglican bishops after their conference the year before, is published by Faber & Faber. Eliot deprecates the bishops' 'tone of excessive amiability' and notes a certain weakness in spiritual authority with regard to such topics as the teaching of Christianity to young people and the practice of birth control; but concludes that 'the Report will have strengthened the Church both within and without'. In this volume he also comments on the reviews which his past work has received. Concerning *The Waste Land*, he writes that it is 'nonsense' that he had expressed 'the disillusionment of a generation', as some critics had suggested; and concerning *For Lancelot Andrewes: Essays on Style and Order*, he writes that the reviewer of *The Times Literary Supplement*, surprised by Eliot's preoccupation with religion, turned his review into: 'a flattering obituary notice. . .to his distress I was unmistakeably making off in the wrong direction'.

April: The April issue of *The Criterion* contains the German novelist Thomas Mann's attack on Nazism, 'An Appeal to Reason', in which he describes its symptoms and ill-effects. Eliot, in his 'Commentary', makes light of current British political parties and notes: 'The Mosley programme (Macmillan: 6d.) though in some respects vague or feeble, contains at least some germs of intelligence.'

15 April: *The Listener* publishes the first of three broadcasts by Eliot on Dryden. They are: 'John Dryden — the Poet who Gave the English Speech' (15 April), 'Dryden the Dramatist' (22 April) and 'Dryden the Critic' (29 April).

July: In his 'Commentary' in *The Criterion*, Eliot recalls the Unitarianism in which he had been brought up: 'things were either black or white.'

19 September: A translation of *Pascal's Pensées* by W. F. Trotter is published by Dent, with an introduction by Eliot. Eliot points out that the Jansenists of Port-Royal, with whom Pascal was associated, constituted 'morally a Puritan movement within the Church', and suggests that Pascal is the Christian writer most pertinent to modern times in his 'unique combination and balance of qualities'.

1 December: Eliot's essay, 'Donne in our Time' appears in *A Garland for John Donne*, edited by Theodore Spencer and published by Harvard University Press. Eliot prophesies that Donne's reputation will continue to increase, not because of the currently fashionable interest in his prose writings or his personality, but because of his innovations in the field of lyric verse. Eliot also recals Professor Briggs' courses in Donne's poetry which he took as an undergraduate at Harvard; although he has forgotten the actual words they were 'enough to attract to private reading at least one Freshman. . . '.

23 December: James Joyce writes to Eliot from Paris to introduce to him one Louis Gillet, who recently wrote on Joyce's work in the *Revue des Deux Mondes*: 'I think you will like to meet him for he is in sympathy with what we are all trying in our different ways to do.'

1932

January: In *The Criterion*, reviewing a book called *This Unemployment*, Eliot states: 'A certain amount of routine, of dullness and of necessity seems inseparable from work; and for myself, I am too sceptical of my own abilities to be able to make a whole-time job of writing poetry, even if I had the means.'

19 February: Eliot writes to George Orwell (Eric Blair) rejecting his manuscript *A Scullion's Diary*, the original title of *Down and Out in Paris and London*, later published by Gollancz in 1933. (Crick, 1980).

March: *Bubu de Montparnasse* by Charles-Louis Philippe, the novel of Paris low life that Eliot read during 1910–11 in Paris, is reprinted by Faber & Faber with a preface by Eliot, who finds that the book still evokes 'an intense pity for the humble and oppressed'.

2 March: Harold Nicolson, the English diplomat, author and critic, records in his *Diaries* (1966) lunching with Eliot and another friend, Jim Barnes, to discuss the compiling of a symposium on modern politics. Nicolson proposes that Barnes should write an introduction to make it plain that the book will be of New Party (founded by Oswald Mosley in 1931) tendencies, but pointing out Mosley's mistakes; to which Eliot agrees. Nicolson describes Eliot as: 'Very yellow and glum. Perfect manners. He looks like a sacerdotal lawyer – dyspeptic, ascetic, eclectic. Inhibitions. Yet obviously a nice man and a great poet.'

16 March: *The Listener* publishes the first of Eliot's four broadcasts entitled 'The Modern Dilemma'. In the first broadcast, 'Christianity and Communism', Eliot says he must have chastity, austerity, humility and sanctity, or perish. The other talks are 'Religion and Science: A Phantom

Dilemma' (23 March), 'The Search for Moral Sanction' (30 March), and 'Building Up the Christian World' (6 April).

May: The first issue of *Scrutiny*, the literary magazine edited by F. R. and Q. D. Leavis, appears; and in an editorial F. R. Leavis writes: 'Let us. . . express now the general regret that the name of *The Criterion* has become so dismal an irony and that the Editor is so far from applying to his contributors the standards we have learnt from him.' During the 1930's *Scrutiny* becomes an opposing pole of opinion to *The Criterion* (descending occasionally to personal abuse), differing from *The Criterion* in that it aims at a specific audience: those teaching and studying English in universities and schools; and a particular set of issues: the way in which the academic study of English literature and the practice of criticism interpenetrates with the realities of mass culture and industrial civilization.

July: The July issue of *The Criterion* contains its first poem by Hugh McDiarmid, 'Second Hymn to Lenin'; and a review by Eliot of Q. D. Leavis's *Fiction and the Reading Public*, in which he expresses his disquiet about the deterioration of the reading taste of the general public. Also in this issue Ezra Pound writes about the shift of style between Eliot's early work and his 'quatrain' poems, first published in *The Little Review* in July 1917 and September 1918: 'two authors, neither engaged in picking the others pocket, decided that the dilution of *vers libre*, Amygism (influence of Amy Lowell). . .general floppiness had gone to far and that some countercurrent must be set going.'

Early autumn.   Having received an invitation to deliver the Charles Eliot Norton lectures at Harvard, Eliot decides to go to the USA without his wife, provoking a deterioration in Vivienne's always precarious mental state. Robert Sencourt recalls (1971) that when Eliot is on his way to Waterloo Station to catch the boat–train, he suddenly finds that Vivienne has hidden some of his most important papers in their flat. The papers are hastily retrieved (a page boy climbs through the bathroom window) and Eliot is able to continue his journey.

15 September: Eliot's *Selected Essays 1917–1932* is published by Faber & Faber.

October: The October issue of *The Criterion* publishes two poems by Louis McNeice. Eliot's 'Commentary', using as starting point Curtius's observation that 'the Permanent has come to mean Paralysis and Death', explores the modern tendency to 'over-estimation of the importance of our own time', and stresses that each age must find its own 'relation of the Eternal and the Transient'. This theme looks forward to Eliot's *The Idea of a Christian Society* (1939) and *Notes towards the Definition of Culture* (1948); and becomes a theme of *Murder in the Cathedral* (1935), *The Cocktail Party* (1950) and the *Four Quartets* (1944).

18 October: Eliot's *John Dryden: The Poet, the Dramatist and the Critic* is published in New York by Terence and Elsa Holliday (reprints of Eliot's three BBC broadcasts of April 1931).

23 October: Eliot arrives in Montreal.

4 November: Eliot delivers his introductory lecture at Harvard. He gives eight lectures altogether, to be published in November 1933 as *The Use of Poetry and the Use of Criticism*. The course of lectures is an attempt to chart the development of critical consciousness from Elizabethan to contemporary times. In the first four lectures Eliot discusses the achievements of Sir Philip Sidney in his criticism of Elizabethan drama, Dryden, and Coleridge. More generally, discussing the processes by which a poet might be formed, Eliot recalls his childhood summers in Massachusetts, and how an object perceived at random, for instance a sea-anemone, might reappear in the poet's mind in later years, 'charged with great imaginative pressure'. Eliot also recalls his schoolboy tastes in poetry, and that Edward Fitzgerald's translation of 'Omar Khayyam' (1859) was 'an almost overwhelming introduction to a new world of feeling' and how he afterwards read Byron, Shelley, Keats, Rossetti and Swinburne. In a passage in which he discusses conditions favourable to poetic inspiration, he seems to be referring to his own experiences in writing 'The Waste Land': 'some forms of ill health, debility or anaemia, may. . .produce an efflux of poetry in a way approaching the condition of automatic writing.'

1 December: Eliot's poem, *Sweeney Agonistes: Fragments of an Aristophanic Melodrama*, is published by Faber & Faber.

1933

January: Eliot's poems, 'Five Finger Exercises', are published in *The Criterion*. This issue also includes a short poem, 'Ecce puer' by James Joyce; a translation of a *Preface to Lady Chatterley's Lover*, by André Malraux; and, in the 'Commentary', some of Eliot's impressions of New York, especially his comments on fashionable 'communistic theories' amongst young intellectuals. (This might be a reference to the left-wing critic, Edmund Wilson, who in *Axel's Castle* (1931) referred to Eliot's 'reactionary point of view'.)

February: Eliot writes to his solicitor instructing him to prepare a Deed of Separation from his wife Vivienne; and from the time of Eliot's return to England they live apart. Vivienne remains in Clarence Gate Gardens until her final breakdown in 1939.

17 February: Eliot resumes his course of Charles Eliot Norton lectures by discussing Shelley and Keats. His attack on Shelley ('some of his views I positively dislike') has been seen by commentators as a reflection of the crisis in his private life. In his remaining lectures ('Matthew Arnold', 'The Modern Mind' and 'Conclusion') Eliot offers a summing-up of the pattern of literary criticism: 'From time to time, every hundred years or so, it is desirable that some critic shall appear to review the past of a literature, and set the poets and the poems in a new order. The task is not one of revolution but of readjustment.' He also suggests, in his last lecture, that 'the ideal medium for poetry' is 'the theatre'.

June: Eliot returns to England. Anxious to avoid London, he stays in a cottage in the grounds of Pikes Farm, Crowhurst, Surrey, where his co-director at Faber & Faber, Frank Morley, lives with his family.

July: *The Criterion* includes 'Freud's Position in the History of Modern Thought' by Thomas Mann, in which Mann reinterprets Freud and defends his thought against the charge of being one of the impulses behind Nazism; 'Two Poems' by W. H. Auden; and 'Murder by Capital' by Ezra Pound, an attack on the economics of 'American capital'. Pound, a disciple of the 'Social Credit' movement for monetary reform, will continue throughout the 1930's to write articles generally considered anti-American and pro-Fascist; culminating in his broadcasts on Rome Radio between 1939 and 1943.

7 August: Frank Morley recalls (Tate, 1967) that when he and his wife returned from holiday: 'The estate was in good heart, and so was Tom. He was sunburnt, but more important, he had been in touch with people he had thought of, and was planning to write *The Rock*.'

Autumn: Eliot returns to the USA, to Charlottesville, to give the Page-Barbour lectures at the University of Virginia, published in 1934 as *After Strange Gods*. These lectures reveal Eliot at his most doctrinaire — he prefers a short story of Joyce's to ones by Katharine Mansfield and D. H. Lawrence on the grounds that it is 'the most ethically orthodox'; accuses Pound, Yeats and even the Jesuit Gerard Manly Hopkins of lack of 'orthodoxy'; and finds that Lawrence and Hardy both express 'some morbid emotion'. He is later (Hall, 1978) to call *After Strange Gods* 'a bad book, a bad book, a bad book'.

In these lectures Eliot also looks back on his student years, recalling how the two years he spent studying Sanskrit left him in 'a state of enlightened mystification'; he withdrew from the classes as he felt he could only penetrate their complexities by ceasing to think as an American or a European, 'which. . .I did not wish to do'.

22 September: Eliot lunches with E. Martin Browne, the director of drama for the Canterbury Festival, to whom he had been introduced by the Bishop of Chichester three years before. During 1933 Browne has been working with the Reverend R. Webb-Odell, on a projected pageant of the history of the church in Britain. (Webb-Odell is the director of an Anglican fund to raise for church-building.) Browne has prepared a draft scenario and asks Eliot if he would be interested in providing words; Eliot enthusiastically accepts. In *The Three Voices of Poetry* (1953) he will recall the stimulating effect this commission had on his writing.

October: In the October issue of *The Criterion* Eliot mourns the death of Irving Babbitt, whose courses he attended at Harvard during 1911/12.

He recalls how Babbitt introduced him to such books as Aristotle's *Politics* and La Fontaine's *Fables*; and the fascination of his lectures, dominated by Babbitt's 'intellectual passion, one might say intellectual fury'. Eliot also discusses Babbitt's ideas on education, expressed in *Literature and the American College* (1908), where Babbitt, in line with other educationalists of the time, opposed the 'credit' system of studying for a degree, introduced at Harvard by Charles Eliot Norton. Here, and in 'The Aims of Education' (1950), Eliot expresses his concern over the deterioration of both the English and American education systems.

Eliot also comments in this issue of *The Criterion* that Ezra Pound is interested in public affairs as an 'artist', whilst he himself considers them 'as a moralist'.

6 October: E. Martin Browne records in his diary that he lunched with Eliot in London and that they visited the Reverend Webb-Odell (see 22 September).

16 October: E. Martin Browne records in his diary 'In London: T. S. Eliot and Lilian Baylis'. Lilian Baylis built up the Old Vic into the people's theatre for Shakespeare and opera, and has also taken over Sadlers Wells, where *The Rock* will be performed.

19 October: The *Christian Register* prints an article by Eliot, 'The Modern Dilemma', originally an address to a meeting of Unitarian clergymen in Boston; in which Eliot recalls his religious background, saying that from Unitarianism he lapsed into agnosticism, and out of agnosticism, after inclining towards Buddhism around 1922, to the Catholic idea which he preferred in its Anglican form.

November: In an article on James Joyce in *The Dial* Eliot calls *Ulysses* 'the most important literary expression of the age'.

2 November: English and American editions appear simultaneously of *The Use of Poetry and the Use of Criticism*.

Towards the end of 1933 Eliot moves into the clergy-house of St Stephen's Church, Gloucester Road, where he will live for the next five or six years. St Stephens is well known for its Anglo-Catholic services, and Eliot becomes Vicar's Warden from 1934 to 1959 — the highest lay position in the parish. In March 1956 he will pay tribute to the vicar of St Stephen's, Father Cheetham, in *The Church Times*.

1934

Early 1934: Eliot's first piece of dramatic writing, *Sweeney Agonistes*, is performed in London at the Group Theatre rooms, produced by Rupert

Doone, a former ballet dancer who had also produced work by W. H. Auden, Christopher Isherwood and Louis MacNeice. Neville Coghill, the Oxford don and literary critic, remembers (March and Tambimuttu, 1948) the opening of *Sweeney Agonistes*: 'About thirty of us were gathered round an almost empty room without a stage, but the almost fabulous figures of Lady Ottoline Morrell, Mr Aldous Huxley and Mr Eliot himself were pointed out to me in a whisper.' Coghill also comments on the brilliance of Doone's performance as Snow: 'As he presented it, it was a study in the psychology of a Crippen; he made it seem that we were all Crippens at heart.'

January: The January issue of *The Criterion* includes 'Four Poems' by Louis MacNeice, and a short parody by Eliot of Winston Churchill's prose style (in 'Commentary').

9 January: Eliot writes to James Joyce that Faber is unable to publish *Ulysses* at the present time; but that he hopes to publish it when the atmosphere is more favourable. (Gilbert, 1957).

22 February: *After Strange Gods: A Primer of Modern Heresy* is published by Faber & Faber.

March/April: Eliot and Pound engage in a correspondence in the *New English Weekly*, following that paper's publication of an unfavourable review by Pound of *After Strange Gods*. Finally, in a letter signed 'Your outraged Possum' Eliot registers his disapproval of the fact that Pound devoted more space to reviewing *After Strange Gods* ('an unsatisfactory attempt to say something worth saying') than to *The Use of Poetry and the Use of Criticism* ('an unsatisfactory attempt to say a variety of things most of which were not worth saying'). The *New English Weekly* is the leading 'Social Credit' paper – expounding the ideas of a Major C. H. Douglas, who claimed that increased prosperity could be achieved by a reform of the monetary system. Its editor is J. R. Orage, described by Eliot as the best leader-writer in London. (Carswell, 1978).

April: In the April issue of *The Criterion*, Eliot recalls the period when he studied in Paris (1910/11), at that time the city of intellectual innovation; mentioning various poets, philosophers and teachers, and how: 'over all swung the spider-like figure of Bergson. His metaphysic was said to throw some light upon the new ways of painting, and discussion of Bergson was apt to be involved with discussion of Matisse and Picasso.' He also briefly but vividly recalls his friend Jean Verdenal, later killed in World War I, and to whom he dedicated *Prufrock and Other Observations* (1917).

The *Virginia Quarterly Review* prints Eliot's poems 'New Hampshire' and 'Virginia'.

28 May: *The Rock: A Pageant Play* opens at the Sadlers Wells Theatre for a two-week run. The pageant enacts the development of the English Church from Roman to contemporary times, using a chorus as narrator-cum-commentator. (This use of the chorus is a device which Eliot will develop further in his next play, *Murder in the Cathedral*.) *The Rock* is a huge production, with 22 scene changes, a cast of over 300 (mostly

amateurs from various London parishes), an orchestra of 40, and a small
choir of picked singers. It attracts an audience of about 1,500 every night.

The play, and more particularly Eliot's choruses, attract much favourable critical notice. *The Times* (29 May) says: 'Mr Eliot's pageant play
looked first to liturgy for its dramatic form, though wisely imitating also
the read and popular stage modes, such as music-hall, ballet and mime . . .
Mr Eliot . . . has created a new thing in the theatre and made smoother the
path towards a contemporary poetic drama.' *The Morning Post* talks of a
'stupendous effort', the *Daily Telegraph* finds it 'no less startling than
The Waste Land in its poetry, its imaginative brilliance and its satirical
force'; *The New Statesman* talks of 'The magnificent verse, the crashing
Hebraic choruses which. . .cannot be fully appreciated after a single
hearing. . . '

31 May: *The Rock* is published by Faber & Faber.

Summer: Eliot receives an invitation from George Bell, Bishop of Winchester, to write a religious poetic drama to be staged in the Chapter House
of Canterbury Cathedral for the Canterbury Festival of the following year.
Eliot will recall his 'gratitude' to Dr. Bell, in *The Times*, 14 October 1958.

July: In his 'Commentary' in the July issue of *The Criterion* Eliot unfavourably reviews *The Modern Muse*, an anthology of modern verse
published by the English Association. He disapproves of the fact that the
poetry has been selected to give a cross-section, rather than according to
standards of excellence, when it might have done something towards
'educating the public taste'.

4 October: Eliot's *Elizabethan Essays* is published by Faber & Faber.

Winter: Before beginning what is to become *Murder in the Cathedral*,
Eliot revisits Canterbury to refresh his memory of the cathedral and its
precincts. Also at about this time he visits friends in Chipping Camden,
Gloucestershire; and together they visit nearby Burnt Norton House, a
Cotswold mansion with fine grounds, later used by Eliot in the first of his
'Four Quartets'.

1935

Early 1935:   Eliot is occupied in finishing *Murder in the Cathedral*, his
play about the martyrdom of Thomas à Becket, for the Canterbury Festival;
in the latter stages with the help and collaboration of E. Martin Browne. In
The New York Times Book Review (29 November 1953), Eliot will discuss
how *Murder in the Cathedral* provided the genesis for his poem, 'Burnt
Norton'.

January: The January issue of *The Criterion* includes an article, 'The Decay of Intelligence in America', by Canon B. Iddings Bell (an American), in which he defines intelligence as power to discriminate and stand out against 'mass judgments', 'Canto XXXVI' by Ezra Pound; and 'The Visitor', a short story by Dylan Thomas.

5 January: In the first of what he calls a series of 'ten-minute lunch-hour sermons', in the independent weekly *Time and Tide*'s 'Notes on the Way', Eliot discusses, amongst other topics, what seems to him 'confused and insufficient thinking about war', with particular reference to a recent book by A. A. Milne, *Peace with Honour*. A heated correspondence with A. A. Milne follows during January and February. Milne accuses Eliot of having made an 'attack on the pacifist's assumptions' and is supported by Rebecca West, who refers to 'the Eliot legend of the Great White Literary Spirit'.

7 March: In a letter to Brenda Salkeld, George Orwell comments on some back numbers of *The Criterion* that he has been reading: 'I must say that for pure snootiness it beats anything I have ever seen'. (Crick, 1980).

April: *Selected Poems* by the American poet Marianne Moore is published in New York by the Macmillan Company, and then in London by Faber & Faber, edited and with an introduction by Eliot in which he states that her poems form 'part of the small body of durable poetry written in our time'.

7 May: Rehearsals of *Murder in the Cathedral* start in Canterbury, with E. Martin Browne as producer. The amateur chorus is trained by Gwyneth Thorborn, principal of the Central School of Speech and Drama, who had also worked on the choruses in *The Rock*.

Thorborn afterwards recalls: 'On one occasion he (Eliot) came up to me during rehearsal and murmured very confidentially "That should be a colon, not a semi-colon". I think this was the only spontaneous remark he ever made in rehearsals.' (Browne, 1969).

6 June: In an article in the *New English Weekly*, Eliot comments that *New Realism*, the book which made such an impact during the period of his philosophy studies at Harvard: 'seems now as demoded as ladies' hats of the same period'. He also recalls the state of American letters around the year 1910, and the apparent lack of a vigorous literary tradition for younger American writers: 'there was literally no-one to whom one would have dreamt of applying'.

15 June: *Murder in the Cathedral* has its first performance in the Chapter House of Canterbury Cathedral, with the Roman Catholic actor Robert Speaight as Becket. It is immediately acclaimed by the critics. *The New Statesman* says: 'Mr. Eliot is to be thanked for having broken away from the naturalistic tradition of historical drama'; the *Daily Telegraph* says: 'How good it is, then, to be able to salute in T. S. Eliot a distinguished man of letters who can use the stage for his purpose while not depriving it of its own quality.' The writer of the 'London Letter' in *The New Yorker* says: 'One's feeling was that here at last was the English language literally being used, itself becoming the stuff of drama, turning alive with its own natural poetry.' The play is also seen by Ashley Dukes, husband of Marie Rambert and owner of the Mercury Theatre in London, which stages experimental drama and ballet. He offers to bring the play to London, which Eliot will recall in *The Times*, 7 May 1959.

October: The October issue of *The Criterion* includes 'Early Poems and Extracts from the Notebooks and Papers' of Gerard Manley Hopkins, the Victorian Jesuit poet. `

1 November: *Murder in the Cathedral* opens in London at the Mercury Theatre. The chorus is drawn from students who have just left the Central School. *The Times* calls *Murder in the Cathedral*: 'The one great play by a contemporary dramatist now to be seen in England.'

29 November: A letter by Eliot on 'Stilton Cheese' is published in *The Times*: 'nothing less is required than the formation of a Society for the Preservation of Ancient Cheeses'.

During 1935, Eliot is a regular contributor to the *New English Weekly*.

1936

5 March: Eliot's *Essays Ancient and Modern* is published by Faber & Faber.

April: The April issue of *The Criterion* includes 'From "Faridun's Poems"' by Basil Bunting. Bunting's later major poem, 'Briggflatts' (1966), will be much influenced by Eliot's 'Four Quartets', though Eliot himself calls Bunting 'too Poundian' (Vinson, 1979).

2 April: Eliot's *Collected Poems, 1909–1935* is published by Faber & Faber. Reviewing the book in *Scrutiny*, D. W. Harding speaks of 'the change in attitude that has made Mr. Eliot's work less *chic* now than it was 10 years ago' and goes on to praise 'Mr. Eliot's amazing genius in the use of words and rhythms and his extraordinary fertility in styles of writing, each "manner" apparently perfected from the first and often used only once (only once, that is, by Mr Eliot, though most are like comets with a string of poetasters laboriously tailing after them).'

May: *Poems of Tennyson* is published by Nelson, with an introduction by Eliot, later published in essay form as 'In Memoriam'. Eliot stresses Tennyson's technical accomplishments, his 'abundance, variety and complete competence'. However, he compares Tennyson's 'Ulysses' unfavourably with canto XXVI of Dante's *Inferno*: 'Dante is telling a story. Tennyson is only stating an elegiac mood.'

July: The July issue of *The Criterion* includes 'The Orchards', a short story by Dylan Thomas, and 'A Year in the Theatre' by drama critic Michael Sayers, which includes an irreverent look at Eliot's own dramatic work during the year. Sayers opines that 'Thomas himself', Thomas à Becket in *Murder in the Cathedral*, 'is a bore most of the time'.

2 July: *Essays and Studies* by Members of the English Association, collected by Herbert Read and published by Oxford University Press, contains Eliot's 'Note on the Verse of John Milton', which Eliot will later regard as an excessively critical view and will modify in his 1947 lecture (26 March).

30 October: *Murder in the Cathedral* transfers from the Mercury Theatre to the larger Duchess Theatre, owned by J. P. Mitchelhill, a real estate agent and admirer of Eliot's work.

25 November. Eliot's article 'The Need for Poetic Drama' is published in *The Listener*. Eliot discusses the functions of a chorus in poetic drama.

21 December: *Murder in the Cathedral* is televized for the BBC.

1937

Early 1937: Mitchelhill discusses with E. Martin Browne taking *Murder in the Cathedral* to the provinces. It will go first to Leeds, then to Manchester and Edinburgh, returning in June for a further five-week London run at the Old Vic.

January: The January issue of *The Criterion* includes an adverse review by Stephen Spender of F. R. Leavis's *Revaluation, Tradition and Development in English Poetry*. In his 'Commentary' Eliot discusses recent events in Spain (the Spanish Civil War started in July 1936) and indicates the shortcomings, in his view, of both the right and the left.

17 February: *The Listener* publishes Eliot's article 'The Church's Message to the World'; in which Eliot defends the rights of the Church 'to affirm, to teach and to apply, true theology'.

18 February: An essay on Byron by Eliot is published in *From Anne to Victoria: Essays by Various Hands*, edited by Bonamy Dobrée. Eliot discusses Byron as a Scottish poet, whose work shows the influence of Calvinist theology, comparing his poetry to that of Burns, Walter Scott and Dunbar. He considers Byron, at his best, a narrative poet ('he added nothing to the language') but praises the last four cantos of 'Don Juan', where Byron's satire on English society is 'very much what an intelligent foreigner in the same position would understand and dislike'.

4 March: *Nightwood*, by Djuana Barnes, an experimental novel set in Paris, is published by Faber & Faber, with a preface by Eliot in which he dismisses the possibility that the book might be considered immoral. More generally, Eliot comments on the shortcomings of the Unitarian morality that he was taught as a boy; and, equally, on the shortcomings of the contemporary notion that 'all individual misery is the fault of "society"'; concluding that: 'all of us, so far as we attach ourselves to created objects and surrender our wills to temporal ends, are eaten by the same worm'.

16 July: In a speech, 'The Ecumenical Nature of the Church', delivered at the Oxford Conference, Eliot calls upon Anglican churchmen for a stricter, more demanding theology.

19–24 July: *Murder in the Cathedral* is performed in Tewkesbury Abbey as part of the Tewkesbury Festival.

Autumn: In 'Religious Drama: Medieval and Modern', published in *The University of Edinburgh Journal*, Eliot says that, to appeal to a modern audience, religious drama must move away from pageantry and become 'something less sedative'. He suggests that 'the most serious plays have always been of deeply religious significance' and expresses the 'dream' that all cathedrals should have their own amateur companies, performing modern religious plays.

October: The October issue of *The Criterion* includes 'Un Etre Etoilque', an article by Henry Miller, the American poet and novelist, on the diaries of Anaïs Nin. Miller and Nin are both living in Paris at this time, and Eliot's contacts with Paris and its literary life are probably reinforced by what he, in an obituary letter on Sylvia Beach in *The Times*, 13 October 1962, calls 'frequent excursions across the Channel'. In the same letter, he remembers dining with Sylvia Beach in Paris at about this period, and that André Gide was amongst the other guests. Sylvia Beach runs the Paris bookshop Shakespeare & Co., a centre of Anglo-American expatriate literary life between the two wars.

14 November: E. Martin Browne records that Eliot read him the first draft of a new play. This goes into several further drafts and is eventually titled *The Family Reunion*.

1938

January: E. Martin Browne and Ashley Dukes take the London production of *Murder in the Cathedral* to the USA, where it has short runs in Boston and New York. Critical reaction is 'interested and appreciative'.

15 February: Eliot writes to E. Martin Browne, in New York with *Murder in the Cathedral*, that he is sending him under separate cover the complete text of *The Family Reunion*. (Browne, 1969).

11 March: E. Martin Browne replies to Eliot that both he and Dukes feel that the play is 'weak in plot', although they are 'enthralled . . . by the skill and wit of the versification'.

19 March: Eliot writes to E. Martin Browne that he is going to Portugal to be one of the judges of the Camoens Prize, also commenting on the tension of the international situation. (Browne, 1969).

April: The Hanging Committee of the Royal Academy of Arts rejects a portrait of Eliot by Wyndham Lewis. This leads to an outcry against the alleged conservatism of the Royal Academy (Augustus John resigns in protest) and the portrait is later bought by the Durban Municipal Art Gallery. Wyndham Lewis paints Eliot's portrait again in 1949 and the second portrait is in Magdalene College, Cambridge.

July: Eliot's article 'Five Points on Dramatic Writing, From a letter to Ezra Pound' is published in *The Townsman*, an avant-garde quarterly on the arts, to which Pound has been a regular contributor. In a playful article written in something of Pound's style, Eliot stresses the importance of keeping the audience's attention, however serious the content of a play; and stresses that: 'the verse (of a play) ought to be a medium to look THROUGH, and not a pretty decoration to look AT!'

4 August: In a letter to *The Times*, Eliot pays tribute to Professor Harold Joachim, under whom he studied at Oxford; saying that it is to Joachim he owes: 'not only whatever knowledge of the philosophy of Aristotle I may once have possessed but also whatever command of prose style I still possess'.

10 August: Eliot visits E. Martin Browne at Stratford-on-Avon to discuss *The Family Reunion*.

September: The 'Munich Crisis'. In a climate of impending international crisis, Neville Chamberlain signs an agreement at Munich with Hitler, and returns to be acclaimed as a saviour of peace. Like many others Eliot feels this to be deeply false; he will comment upon these feelings in his lectures at Corpus Christi College, Cambridge, in March 1939.

October: In his 'Commentary' in *The Criterion*. Eliot expresses a characteristic lack of faith in party politics as capable of providing any solution in the current crisis. 'There seems no hope in contemporary politics at all.'

During October E. Martin Browne notes that he worked on *The Family Reunion* with Eliot.

9 October: Eliot writes to E. Martin Browne that he is anxious to complete a final draft of *The Family Reunion* as soon as possible, so that it can be published at the same time as the play is produced. In the future, Eliot sends his plays to press after the opening night, allowing him to incorporate any changes made during rehearsals and after the first audience-reaction.

December: *The Harvard Advocate* reprints Eliot's past contributions with the title 'The Undergraduate Poems of T. S. Eliot' (including 'Ode').

Robert Lowell, the eminent American poet, then a Harvard freshman, calls Eliot 'a tireless Calvinist' who 'harries his pagan English public with godliness and austerity'.

1939

January: The last issue of *The Criterion* appears. In his editorial 'Last Words', Eliot speaks of a 'feeling of staleness' in himself, caused partly by the impending political crisis: 'I no longer feel the enthusiasm necessary to make a literary review what it should be', also indicating a development in his own thinking – 'a right political philosophy came more and more to imply a right theology' which might be inappropriate to the editor of a literary review. Eliot also looks back on the magazine's history, recalling the time when it appeared as a monthly, when he decided that 'whatever editorial talent I possessed did not extend to the preparation of a review appearing oftener than four times a year'. He goes on to mention the July 1929 issue, with its short story competition, as a kind of realization of what he wanted to achieve, and regretting that, after this date: 'The "European Mind" which one had mistakenly thought might be renewed and fortified, disappeared from view. . .Here in England, a definitely postwar generation began to speak.' In his March 1946 broadcast, 'The Unity of European Culture', Eliot will also describe a narrowing of scope in *The Criterion*, forced on him by various political and intellectual factors in Europe.

15 February: E. Martin Browne reads the final text of *The Family Reunion*, after it has undergone extensive revisions. The theme of the play is taken from Aeschylus' *Choephoroi*, in which Orestes is hunted down by the Furies; Eliot places it in a contemporary setting, dramatizing a contemporary pattern of family relationships.

20 February: Rehearsals of *The Family Reunion* begin, with Michael Redgrave in the part of Harry, Helen Haye as Amy and Catherine Lacey as Agatha. Eliot later tells Walter Turner Levy (Levy and Scherle, 1968) that John Gielgud wanted the part of Harry, but that he (Eliot) was unwilling, feeling that Gielgud would not fully understand the religious motivation of the character.

March: Eliot delivers three lectures at Corpus Christi College, Cambridge, published in October as *The Idea of a Christian Society*. He discusses the theme that: 'the only hopeful course for a society which would thrive and continue its creative activity in the arts of civilisation, is to become Christian.' He also describes the very deep perturbation he felt during the Munich Crisis of September 1938; what he felt was: 'not. . .a criticism of the government, but a doubt of the validity of a civilisation'.

21 March: *The Family Reunion* opens at the Westminster Theatre, to mixed reviews. Charles Morgan of *The Times* salutes Eliot's 'bold experiment in language' but says 'sad to say, the good will just fails in this case to get warmed into enthusiasm'. The *Daily Sketch* praises 'a new and important and profoundly interesting contribution to English drama'; the *Daily Telegraph* finds it 'a deeply interesting, though difficult evening'. James Agate of *The Sunday Times*, writes his review in a pastiche of Eliot and seems to be suggesting he finds Eliot's style mannered and willfully obscure.

In *Poetry and Drama* (1951) Eliot will discuss the uncertainty he felt about *The Family Reunion*.

April: Eliot is made an honorary Fellow of Magdalene College, Cambridge.

July/September: *Purpose* publishes Chapter 1 of *The Idea of a Christian Society*.

3 September: Britain declares war on Germany. Stephen Spender later says of Eliot that: 'The war modified his attitude by convincing him that there was a Western cause to be positively defended. And after the war there was a Germany to be brought back within the Western tradition.' (Spender, 1975).

Because of the bombing Eliot moves from the clergy house of St Stephens to Shamley Green, near Richmond in Surrey, where he lives as the guest of Mrs. Mirrlees, the mother of the poet Hope Mirrlees. He continues to work at Faber & Faber on Tuesdays and Wednesdays. 'East Coker', the second of Eliot's 'Four Quartets', is written during the first few months of the war.

5 October: Eliot's *Old Possum's Book of Practical Cats*, his perenially popular collection of humorous doggerel verse inspired by his favourite household pets, is published by Faber & Faber.

26 October: Eliot's *The Idea of a Christian Society* is published by Faber & Faber.

7 December: The *Queen's Book of the Red Cross* is published, with two contributions by Eliot, 'The Marching Song of the Pollicle Dogs' and 'Billy M'Caw: The Remarkable Parrot'.

During 1939: *Noctes Binanianae*, a collection of light verse, written and exchanged by Geoffrey Faber, Frank Morley, T. S. Eliot and John Hayward, is privately published, commemorating a series of evenings held by John Hayward at his flat in Bina Gardens. Eliot's contributions include 'How to Pick a Possum' dedicated to Geoffrey Faber. Hayward is a bibliophile and anthologist who has been an occasional contributor to *The Criterion*; after the war Eliot lives in his flat in Cheyne Walk.

Although *The Criterion* ended publication in 1939, Eliot's involvement and interest in periodicals continues. In 1939 Eliot is on the board of the *Christian News Letter*; three of his 'four Quartets' have their first publication in the *New English Weekly*; and he encourages younger editors of periodicals, e.g. Cyril Connolly, who starts *Horizon* in 1939.

1940

February: Eliot's *The Waste Land and Other Poems* is published by Faber & Faber.

21 March: The second of Eliot's 'Four Quartets', 'East Coker', is published in the Easter number of the *New English Weekly*, whose editor, Philip Mairet (successor to A. R. Orage) will pay tribute to Eliot's 'princely largesse to voluntary journalism in a cultural cause' (Braybrooke, 1958). East Coker is the village in Somerset from which Eliot's ancestor, Andrew Eliot, emigrated to New England in 1669. *The Times Literary Supplement* reviews 'East Coker' unfavourably, regretting Eliot's 'headshaking' and finding it 'a hymn of humility, but a sad one, and somewhat incongruous'.

June: Eliot goes to Dublin to deliver the first annual Yeats lecture to the Friends of the Irish Academy at the Abbey Theatre. The subject of the lecture is 'The Poetry of W. B. Yeats'; Eliot also comments implicitly on his own work by discussing the options available to a poet in middle age: to stop writing poetry completely, to start to repeat oneself, or to work in a completely different way.

14 August: Eliot becomes guest editor of *The Christian Newsletter* for three weeks.

September/October: The American critic Lionel Trilling reviews *The Idea of a Christian Society* in the *Partisan Review*. He says that although Eliot may have deceived himself in considering the Church an effective force for social reform, he has at least suggested a solution favouring morality and human dignity.

28 November: *The Listener* publishes 'The Writer as Artist: A Discussion' between Eliot and Desmond Hawkins; in which Eliot stresses the importance of the writer in his capacity to 'prevent the language from deteriorating or from getting ossified'.

December: Cyril Connolly, writing in *Horizon* about the difficulties of running a literary magazine, mentions Eliot, as well as E. M. Forster and Desmond MacCarthy, as eminent men of letters who have given the magazine favourable publicity in newspapers or on the radio.

Winter 1940/41:   During the bombing of London, Eliot serves as a fire-watcher on the roof of the Faber & Faber offices, an experience drawn on for Part II of 'Little Gidding'. He later describes to Walter Turner Levy (Levy and Scherle, 1968) how: 'during the Blitz the accumulated debris was suspended in the London air for hours after a bombing. Then it would slowly descend and cover one's sleeves and coat with a fine white ash.'

1941

Early 1941:   Eliot joins with J. H. Oldham, the editor of *The Christian Newsletter*, in a symposium of broadcast talks, 'The Church Looks Ahead'. At about this time Eliot comes into contact with the St Anne's Society, centred on the parish church of St Anne's, Soho, whose purpose is to strengthen the Church's influence and leadership. Other writers attending its meetings include Dorothy Sayers, Rose Macaulay, John Betjeman, C. S. Lewis and David Cecil.

20 February: *Burnt Norton* is published by Faber & Faber.

27 February: 'The Dry Salvages', the third of Eliot's 'Four Quartets', is published in the *New English Weekly*. The title refers to a group of dangerous rocks off the coast of East Gloucester, Massachusetts, where Eliot spent summers as a child and young man. *The Times Literary Supplement* comments: 'A new note has crept into this poetry, a note of quiescence, even of bleak resignation. But it has lost that spice of wit which was woven into the logic of the earlier pieces.'

March: As *The Times* had earlier rejected his letter concerning James Joyce's obituary, Eliot writes another letter to the editor of the paper; it is subsequently published in the Marsh issue of *Horizon*. Eliot considers much of the information contained in the obituary, for example about Joyce's family, irrelevant; and its literary judgements old-fashioned.

10 April: In 'Towards a Christian Britain' printed in *The Listener*, Eliot states that the ambition to create a Christian Britain is: 'the greatest we can take to ourselves'.

April/May: The poet Sidney Keyes, an undergraduate at Oxford, tries to find a publisher for a collection of poetry written by Oxford students since the outbreak of war. Eliot refuses it for Faber but suggests he offers it to Herbert Read, at this time in charge of the poetry list at the publishers Routledge. Keyes comments (Guenter, 1967): 'Eliot and Read work together on all new poetry . . . they share it out.' Keyes will be killed in Tunis in 1943; Read subsequently publishes volumes by both him and his friend John Heath-Stubbs.

May: Eliot contributes to 'Reminiscences of Virginia Woolf' in *Horizon*; Virginia Woolf having committed suicide in March 1941. Eliot's short piece surprises many by its lack of warmth — Eliot comments, not on any of her novels, but on the shortcomings of her biography of Roger Fry and her position at the centre of the Bloomsbury circle.

22 May: Eliot's 'Defence of the Islands' is printed in *Britain at War*, a catalogue of photographs and paintings published by the Museum of Modern Art in New York, to commemorate their exhibition of the same name.

July: Eliot writes to E. Martin Browne, who has been urging him to write another play, that he is working on the poem which becomes 'Little Gidding' but that he hopes his next piece of work will be a play. (Browne, 1969).

24 July: A book of Eliot's essays, *Points of View*, is published by Faber & Faber. This is a selection edited, with Eliot's approval, by John Hayward. It contains 'representative passages' and is designed as an introduction to Eliot's prose work.

3 September: Eliot is guest editor of *The Christian Newsletter*. His reflections on the French Vichy government in this issue have sometimes been taken as a support of its ideology, but Eliot deplores its enactment of anti-Semitic laws and hopes Christians will speak out against them in France.

4 September: *The Dry Salvages* is published by Faber & Faber.

5 September: *Irving Babbitt: Man and Teacher* is published in the USA by Putnam, containing a memoir by Eliot.

13 November: *The Church Looks Ahead* is published by Faber & Faber.

10 December: A letter by Eliot on the subject of 'Russian Ballet' is printed in *The Times*, supporting John Masefield's plea, in a previous letter, that the British public should be allowed to see new ballets and dancers from Russia. Eliot also suggests that the dancers of the Sadlers Wells company should be exempt from national service.

11 December: *A Choice of Kipling's Verse*, selected by Eliot and with an introduction by him, is published by Faber & Faber. Eliot states that the purpose of his essay is to encourage people to read Kipling with fresh eyes; he rejects the prevalent view of Kipling as a 'mere writer of jingles' and makes a comparison between Kipling and Dryden, calling them classical rather than romantic poets.

1942

24 February: Eliot delivers 'The Music of Poetry', the third W. P. Ker Memorial Lecture, at Glasgow University; it will be published by Jackson, Son and Company later in the year. The lecture is an interesting background to Eliot's thoughts while writing the last of the 'Four Quartets': 'the poet is occupied with frontiers of consciousness beyond which words fail, though meanings still exist.'

15 April: Eliot delivers *The Classics and the Man of Letters* as the Presidential Address to the Classical Association; it will be published by Oxford University Press later in the year. He stresses that the classics should continue to be taught in the school curriculum; and discusses the theme that 'the maintenance of classical education is essential to the maintenance of the continuity of English literature'.

Summer: In the Summer issue of *Scrutiny* F. R. Leavis comments that after the publication of the first three 'Quartets', 'it should by now be impossible to doubt that he (Eliot) is among the greatest poets of the English language'.

  Eliot makes a five-week visit to Sweden in the company of George Bell, Bishop of Chichester; visiting Stockholm and the university towns of Lund, Uppsala and Gothenburg. The main purpose of the visit is to make contact with Swedish Christians. (Sencourt, 1971).

15 October: 'Little Gidding', the last of Eliot's 'Four Quartets', is published in the *New English Weekly*. The title refers to the Huntingdonshire village where Nicholas Ferrar, the divine and friend of the poet George Herbert, founded a religious community in the seventeenth century, a period of central importance, both emotionally and imaginatively, to Eliot. *The Times Literary Supplement* is cool in its evaluation: Eliot's theme is 'impressive' but 'tends to reduce the music of poetry to the dry discourse of the moralist and the intellectual'.

23 October: *Introducing James Joyce*, a selection by Eliot of Joyce's prose, is published by Faber & Faber. Eliot's choice of extracts is 'The Sisters' (from *The Dubliners*), and short passages from *Portrait of the Artist as a Young Man, Ulysses* and *Finnegan's Wake*; he explains that these selections have followed 'an autobiographical thread', in that he has taken 'passages in which the author was present either as child or as young man, either as observer or asprotagonist'.

1 December: *Little Gidding* is published by Faber & Faber.

1943

21 January: The *New English Weekly* publishes the first of four articles by Eliot under the heading 'Notes Towards a Definition of Culture'. The others appear on 28 January, 4 and 11 February. The specific points of these articles are generally considered to be hard to follow – in an interview in *John O'London's Weekly*, August 1949, Eliot will comment on their 'obscurity' – but generally, Eliot seems to be elaborating on the fact that: 'The development of culture and the development of religion . . . cannot be clearly isolated from each other'.

22 February: In his *Diaries* (1966), Harold Nicolson records dining with a group of British and Americans, including Eliot. Discussion revolves round a possible threat of Russian supremacy after the war, and how Stalin might be using the war for his own tactical purposes. Nicolson records that Eliot thinks that the best protection for the smaller powers would be 'a great international federation'.

18 March: Eliot delivers a speech 'Civilization: The Nature of Cultural Relations' at an Anglo-Swedish Society luncheon; it will be published in the autumn by the Anglo-Swedish Society with two other speeches, by Lord Sempill and Harold Nicolson. Eliot hopes to see after the war an increase in cultural relations: 'Every country needs to know the best thought, art and science of other countries in order to maintain and develop its own'; and notes that 'the history of European civilisation is a history of perpetual cross-fertilisation'.

14 April: Harold Nicolson records in his *Diaries* (1966) that Eliot participated in a poetry reading organized by Osbert and Edith Sitwell in aid of the Free French. Other poets reading include John Masefield, the poet laureate; Edmund Blunden, and Nicolson's wife, Vita Sackville-West. During the interval the poets are presented to Queen Elizabeth, consort of King Goerge VI.

29 April.   Eliot writes to E. Martin Browne that he would like to write a play, but that he is very preoccupied with the current controversy over the South India Scheme for Church Union. A pamphlet by Eliot on this subject will be published in November. (Browne, 1969).

11 May.   Eliot's four poems, 'Burnt Norton', 'East Coker', 'The Dry Salvages' and 'Little Gidding' are published together in the USA for the first time, as the *Four Quartets*, by Harcourt Brace & Company; it will be published in the UK in October 1944.

Summer: The Summer issue of *Scrutiny* prints a debate on the merits of 'Little Gidding'. D. W. Harding reviews it favourably ('for me it ranks among the major good fortunes of our time that so superb a poet is writing'), R. N. Higinbotham calls Harding's review 'an exposition, almost a paraphrase, but hardly a criticism' and mentions a 'stock-response' and 'the unevenness and lack of homogeneity in these four poems'; finally Leavis defends Harding's account of the poem, recommending 'much attentive re-reading of the whole sequence' and also 'meditation and disciplined self-searching'.

4 June.   In an article in *Tribune*, George Orwell defends Eliot against charges of being right-wing by suggesting the impossibility of judging a writer by any political label (Shakespeare is 'reactionary in tendency'): 'Eliot, in particular, is damned in the left-wing press almost as automatically and perfunctorily as Kipling.' Orwell notes that: 'In its attitude towards "highbrows" . . . the Left is no friendlier than the Right.'

22 July: *Queen Mary's Book for India* is published, containing the poem 'To the Indians who died in Africa', by Eliot.

In his *Diaries* (1966), Harold Nicolson records dining with Sybil Colefax, other guests including Eliot, Stephen Spender and the Duchess of Devonshire. Eliot 'is in a charming mood'.

November: *Reunion by Destruction: Reflections on a Scheme for Church Unity in South India* by Eliot is published as a pamphlet by the Council for the Defence of Church Principles. Eliot discusses a current ecclesiastical controversy over the projected Church of South India, to be formed by a union of the Anglican and Methodist churches. Eliot considers the scheme untenable; as an Anglo-Catholic, he objects to the role of bishops in the proposed body, and considers that the Apostolic Succession will not be properly safeguarded.

November: *The Norseman* publishes 'The Social Function of Poetry,' an extract from a lecture given by Eliot at the British-Norwegian Institute in London. Eliot discusses the duty of the poet: 'his direct duty is to his *language*, first to preserve, and second to extend and improve.'

1944

11 April: Writing to Eliot whilst staying in St Louis, Eliot's birthplace, Wyndham Lewis thanks him for a letter (unpublished) describing his wartime life in London. Lewis comments that Eliot's time seems to be 'packed with official duties', and reports that, whilst Eliot's grandfather is still remembered in St Louis, Eliot himself seems to have been forgotten; although a local college performed *Murder in the Cathedral* the previous Christmas.

17 April: A letter from Eliot on the subject of 'Aristocracy' is published in *The Times*. He suggests that the original meaning of the word has been distorted, and that 'government by the best men is surely the aspiration of every society, whatever its social organisation'.

8 May: In a letter to *The Times* about 'Books for the Freed World', Eliot writes in support of the poet Archibald MacLeish's proposals for international lending libraries after the war, but cautions against any imposition of a different culture: 'It is for the liberated nations to replace or restore as they choose; we should aim only to help them to do which ever they prefer.'

15 June: In an interview in *La France Libre*, entitled 'What France Means to You', Eliot says that if he had not discovered Baudelaire, and the lineage of Baudelairian poets (including Laforgue), he believes he would not have become a writer.

13 July: George Orwell receives a letter from Eliot at Faber & Faber, rejecting *Animal Farm*, also previously rejected by Gollancz and Cape. Eliot praises the quality of the writing, but considers the book's message unhelpful in the current political situation. He adds, in what has been seen by some as evidence of Eliot's 'élitism': 'after all, your pigs are far more intelligent than the other animals, and therefore the best qualified to run the farm. . . what was needed (someone might argue) was not more communism but more public-spirited pigs.' (Crick, 1980).

July/August: In Eliot's essay, 'The Responsibility of the Man of Letters in the Cultural Restoration of Europe', published in *The Norseman*, Eliot calls upon men of letters to be particularly attentive to the conduct of politicians and economists, at a time when their 'decisions and actions . . . are likely to have cultural consequences'.

26 September: Eliot delivers an address, 'What is Minor Poetry?' before the Association of Bookmen of Swansea and West Wales; printed in the *Welsh Review* in December. Eliot offers no definition, but discusses, generally, the formation of literary taste and the constant changes in any poetic reputation, finishing by describing some of his experiences in selecting poetry for publication.

Eliot also delivers the Ballard-Matthews lecture at University College, Bangor, on 'Johnson as Critic and Poet'. Including Dryden and Coleridge as well, Eliot speaks of poets who were also critics, stressing how, as they were all interested in 'a particular kind of poetry', a study of their poetry is relevant to a study of their criticism.

16 October: Eliot delivers an address, 'What is a Classic?' at the Virgil Society; he argues that Virgil, like Dante, is a classic writer, by virtue of his 'maturity' in mind, manners and language, produced when both language and society are at a 'mature' stage; he is also 'a classic ideal' to a Europe suffering the horrors of war.

31 October: The first British edition of Eliot's *Four Quartets* is published by Faber & Faber.

1945

25 January: 'Four Quartets' is printed in the *New English Weekly*.

29 March: In a correspondence in the *New English Weekly* about the 'German mind', Eliot says that he finds German philosophical thought of great value, because he usually disagrees with it; citing Karl Mannheim as an example. This view of Mannheim is also expressed in Eliot's obituary letter on Mannheim to *The Times*, 25 January 1947.

May: Following a series of pro-Fascist broadcasts on Rome Radio between 1939 and 1943, Ezra Pound is arrested for treason against the US government and is imprisoned first in Genoa, then in Pisa. When Eliot hears of Pound being taken into custody he writes to leading literary figures asking them to sign an appeal on Pound's behalf. (Stock, 1970).

July/August: In an obituary letter on Sylvia Beach (*The Times*, 13 October 1962) Eliot will recall visiting Sylvia Beach and Adrienne Monnier, the French translator of *The Love Song of J. Alfred Prufrock*, in Paris, shortly after peace has been declared.

October: Eliot's 'The Class and the Elite' is published in the *New English Weekly*; a revised version of which will become Chapter II of *Notes Towards a Definition of Culture* (1948). Eliot discusses the different social components of a society, which he sees as, ideally, hierarchical: an aristocracy has an 'essential function', though 'the primary channel of transmission is the family'.

17 October: Vita Sackville-West writes to her husband Harold Nicolson, expressing her fears that she is 'out of touch' with contemporary poetry: 'I see that the influence of Tom Eliot and the Spender-Auden school is paramount'.

30 October: In a letter to *The Times* on 'Mass Deportations', Eliot expresses his agreement with Bertrand Russell, who in previous correspondence has pleaded that the Germans in Great Britain ought not to be automatically sent back to Germany, as prevailing conditions there are so bad.

November/December: Ezra Pound is flown to Washington for trial on charges of treason; however he is declared insane and mentally unfit for trial, and is committed to St Elizabeths Hospital, an insane asylum, in Washington D.C.

December: Eliot travels to the USA, his first visit for 13 years, and visits Pound at St Elizabeths Hospital. He will continue to visit him regularly and campaign for his release.

From 1945 onwards, Eliot will visit the USA almost yearly until his death, to give lectures and poetry readings.

1946

10 March: Eliot gives the first of three broadcasts on the BBC's German service, to be collected under the heading 'The Unity of European Culture', which will be published as an appendix to *Notes Towards the Definition of Culture* (1948). The other two lectures are given on 17 and 24 March. Eliot stresses the common cultural heritage of Germany and Great Britain, which includes the Germanic foundation of the English language and the literature of Greece and Rome, as well as the Bible. He describes how in his editorship of *The Criterion*, he became increasingly conscious of 'the gradual closing of the mental frontiers of Europe' and appeals to all European men of letters to preserve 'these goods of which we are the common trustees'. During these broadcasts, Eliot also recalls his studies of ancient Indian languages as a graduate student at Harvard, acknowledging that 'my own poetry shows the influence of Indian thought and sensibility'.

September: *Poetry* prints 'Ezra Pound' by Eliot. Eliot acknowledges his enormous personal debt to Pound, as an editor of 'critical genius' on 'The Waste Land', and also offers an astute defence of Pound, recently committed to a mental asylum: 'Pound was always a masterly judge of poetry; a more fallible judge, I think, of men'. Eliot suggests that it was Pound who brought American poetry into the European mainstream, by creating ' "a modern movement in poetry", in which English and American poets collaborated, knew each other's works, and influenced each other'; and finishes by recalling the American literary scene during the time of his undergraduate studies at Harvard: 'The question was still: where do we go from Swinburne? And the answer appeared to be, nowhere.' (Cf Eliot's article in the *New English Weekly*, 6 June 1935).

31 October: Eliot's play, *The Family Reunion*, is revived at the Mercury Theatre in London, where it runs until February 1947. The critics give it a more favourable reception than at its first showing in 1939. *Punch* talks of: 'verse forms which combine flexibility with impelling rhythms of their own'; the *New Statesman* praises the Chorus: 'The chorus of uncles and aunts is full of individuality, yet with the slightest side-step they fall naturally into the function of chorus'. *Time and Tide* calls it 'a great and important play' and the *New English Weekly* 'incomparably the best modern play now running in London'.

19 December: Eliot's *The Significance of Charles Williams* is printed in the *Listener*. Eliot points out the wide range in the work of this Christian writer, who died the previous year, describing him as a man who: 'was able to live in the material and spiritual world at once, a man to whom the two worlds were equally real because they are one world.' Stephen Medcalf suggests (Vinson, 1979) that Williams' novel *Descent into Hell* (1937) with its theme of the Doppelganger of spiritual double, influenced Eliot in 'Little Gidding' and *The Cocktail Party*.

During 1946 Eliot takes a room in John Hayward's flat in Cheyne Walk, Chelsea, where he lives until his second marriage in January 1957.

1947

23 January: Vivienne, Eliot's divorced wife, dies in a nursing-home, after years of mental illness. The Fabers accompany Eliot to Pinner, Middlesex, for her funeral.

25 January: An obituary letter by Eliot, on Professor Karl Mannheim, is printed in *The Times*. Eliot stresses Mannheim's influence on those who knew him and heard him speak in person: 'Many must be aware of a debt to him, whose points of view are very different from his'.

26 March: Eliot gives 'Milton', the annual lecture of the Henrietta Hertz Trust, to the British Academy; it will be published by Oxford University Press in October. Modifying the opinions he expressed on Milton in July 1936, Eliot says that, now Milton is less of a poetic influence, he feels he can be studied for his technical mastery: 'In comparison with Milton, hardly any subsequent writer of blank verse appears to exercise any freedom at all.'

Summer: The Gateway Theatre in Edinburgh invites E. Martin Browne to produce *Murder in the Cathedral* and *The Family Reunion* for performance at the first Edinburgh festival.

3 June: Eliot gives an address, 'On Poetry', on the occasion of the twenty-fifth anniversary of Concord Academy in Massachusetts. He says that for a poet 'humility is the most essential virtue' and goes on to voice his fears that 'nothing I have written is really of permanent value' and that 'I shall never again write anything good'.

During this trip to the USA Eliot repeats his second lecture on Milton before an auditorium in the Frick Collection in New York; he is also awarded an honorary degree at Harvard.

20 September: In a letter to *The Times* on 'UNESCO and the Philosopher', Eliot expresses his doubts on the recently stated objectives of UNESCO – 'international co-operation in education, science and culture'. Eliot asks: 'How is the term culture to be interpreted? I had always understood culture to comprehend education and science, as well as other interests.'

28 September: E. Martin Browne writes to Eliot that the production of his two plays at the Gateway Theatre in Edinburgh has been very successful; and invites Eliot to write a new play for the following year's Festival.

December: Eliot's choice of 'Books of the Year' is printed in *Horizon*. Excluding any Faber books, he names *The Apostolic Ministry*, by K. E. Kirk and others, and *Christ, The Christian and the Church*, by Mascall.

1948

January: Eliot receives the Order of Merit from George VI.

25 January: Eliot writes to E. Martin Browne that he expects to start a new play during 1948, but does not envisage it being finished before the spring of 1949. (Browne, 1969).

7 May: In a letter to *The Times* on 'Naturalized Subjects', Eliot comments on previous correspondence in which nationalized subjects (of whom he is one) have complained about having to carry their passports with them. Eliot states that he always carries his passport with him, and cannot understand: 'why any naturalized subject should object, or why he should wish to conceal this information, unless he is the sort of person who has something to conceal.'

1 June: Eliot sends E. Martin Browne the first draft of three scenes of a new play.

15 June: E. Martin Browne records in his diary that he and Eliot discussed the first draft of a play called *One-Eyed Riley*, later retitled *The Cocktail Party*.

July: Eliot's *Selected Poems* is published by Penguin Books in association with Faber & Faber; a selection made by Eliot from his *Collected Poems 1909–1935* and containing all his major poetry except 'Four Quartets'. It is published in an edition of 50,000 copies, a huge print-run for a volume of poetry.

28 July: Walter Turner Levy visits Eliot in his office at Faber & Faber and later recalls that they discussed Eliot's play, *The Family Reunion*. Eliot says that he is 'very fond of some of the poetry in it' but thinks of it as 'a failure as a play'. (Levy and Scherle, 1968).

August: Eliot having been unable to complete his new play in time for the Edinburgh Festival, E. Martin Browne produces Christopher Fry's *The Firstborn*, another verse drama by a contemporary playwright.

September: To mark Eliot's sixtieth birthday, a number of distinguished contributors put together *T. S. Eliot: A Symposium*, edited by Richard March and Tambimuttu.
    Eliot travels to the USA to take up a place at the Institute for Advanced Study at Princeton.

18 October: *All Hallows' Eve*, by Charles Williams, is published by Pellegrini & Cudahy, New York, with an introduction by Eliot.

3 November: Eliot delivers the War Memorial Address at Milton Academy, his old school.

5 November: Eliot's *Notes towards the Definition of Culture* is published by Faber & Faber. Bernard Bergonzi comments: 'The book's excessively tentative title is characteristic; Eliot says many interesting things about culture but he never succeeds in defining it. In principle, he is concerned with culture in the broad or anthropological sense . . . In practice, however, Eliot slides from one sense of culture to another in a quite disconcerting way.' (Bergonzi, 1972).
    Following the announcement that Eliot has won the Nobel Prize for Literature, *The Times* notes in its leader that this, and other recent awards, 'display a touch of happy irony, for it is not so many years since MR. ELIOT was the object of general criticism as an opaque and wilful poet with an ancillary talent, not always well employed, for prose criticism.'

The Times adds that Eliot is 'widely considered the chief formative influence in the language at present' and talks of 'a coherence of outlook reflected by an exceptional sense of responsibility'.

19 November: Eliot delivers a lecture at the Library of Congress in Washington, entitled 'From Poe to Valéry', in which he talks of Poe's 'negligible' influence in Britain and the USA and his 'immense' influence on three French poets: Baudelaire, Mallarmé and especially Valéry.

November/December: Eliot leaves the USA for the Nobel Prize-giving ceremony. Robert Giroux, Eliot's American publisher, recalls (Tate, 1967) that when Eliot is asked by reporters for which book he has been awarded the prize, he replies 'the entire corpus', afterwards remarking to Giroux, 'It really might make a good title for a mystery — *The Entire Corpus.*'

10 December: Eliot is presented with the Nobel Prize in Stockholm.

During 1948 Eliot dines with the King and Queen, and is received in private audience by Pope Pius XII (who discourses to Eliot on poetry's relation to religion).

1949

4 January: Hugh Hunt, the new director of the Old Vic, writes to E. Martin Browne about a possible production of *The Cocktail Party* at the Old Vic. He explains that he cannot allow the play to be tied to a particular producer, i.e. E. Martin Browne. Browne conveys this information to Eliot.

6 January: Eliot replies to Browne that he has no hesitation in turning down Hunt's offer, both from 'self-interest', since he has always felt that E. Martin Browne was the only suitable producer for his plays, and 'loyalty'. (Browne, 1969).

20 February: The Library of Congress in Washington announce that Pound's *Pisan Cantos*, written during his detention in Pisa, has won the annual Bollingen Prize for poetry. This decision, made by the Fellows of American Letters, who include Eliot, W. H. Auden, Conrad Aiken and Robert Lowell, causes much controversy.

15 March: E. Martin Browne receives from Eliot the first complete version of *The Cocktail Party*.

May: Eliot is made an Honorary Fellow of Merton College, Oxford.

30 May: *Time* magazine reviews an exhibition of Wyndham Lewis' paintings at the Redfern Gallery in London, where his two portraits of Eliot are on display. Eliot tells the *Time* reporter that there are equally good reasons for sticking to the same painter, as for sticking to the same doctor.

19 August: An interview with Eliot is printed in *John O'London's Weekly*, headed 'T. S. Eliot Answers Questions'. Eliot comments on his book *Notes Towards the Definition of Culture*: 'As for the obscurity, it is difficult for me to say how far I have or have not mastered my own thought'; on *The Four Quartets*: 'the obscurity there is inherent in the ideas expressed'; on his standards in criticism: 'What I seem to have accomplished in criticism is to have altered emphases and revived interest in certain writers'; and on the fact that religion is an inseparable part of his thought: 'Why has an elephant four legs? Religion is the most important element in life and it is in the light of religion that one understands anything.'

22 August: Eliot's play, *The Cocktail Party*, opens at the Lyceum Theatre, Edinburgh, as part of the Edinburgh Festival; produced by E. Martin Browne, with Alec Guinness as Sir Henry Harcourt Reilly. Eliot later tells Walter Turner Levy (Levy and Scherle, 1968) that Guinness, with his 'irrepressible Irish humor' was 'the ideal realization of the part I had written'. *The Times* says: 'In this brilliantly entertaining analysis of problems long since staled by conventional treatment Mr. Eliot achieves a remarkable refinement of his dramatic style.' *The Daily Mail* calls it 'a bewildering muddle of a play, but in many respects a brilliant one'. *The Daily Telegraph* calls it 'one of the finest dramatic achievements of our time'. Against this, *The News Chronicle* calls it 'nothing but a finely acted piece of flapdoodle,' and Ivor Brown in *The Observer* describes the audience reactions: 'The Eliotains were saying it was just too marvellous, and the Oppositions were observing that it was all pretentious mystification and a blether of words.'

27 August: Eliot is interviewed in *The Glasgow Herald*: 'Mr. Eliot smiled when it was suggested to him yesterday that Festival audiences had not found his meaning very plain. "Perhaps," he said gently, "I did not intend that they should." ' Eliot also comments in the interview: 'I would not want to say to anyone that this or that is the meaning (of the play), because the whole interest of the process is in getting your own meaning out of it.'

Autumn: Accompanied by the historian, Arnold Toynbee, Eliot makes a six-week lecture tour of Germany, taking as his theme the problems of European unity. He speaks first at Hamburg, then Berlin, Hanover, Brunswick, Göttingen, Bonn, Frankfurt and Heidelberg, ending the tour at Munich. He speaks of the unity of the European cultural tradition as essential to Europe's progress; and the importance of Christian tradition in Europe. Eliot also visits the University of Münster, where his friend Josef Pieper is professor of philosophy. In 1952 Faber & Faber will publish a translation of Pieper's *Leisure: The Basis of Culture*, with an introduction by Eliot.

September: *New Alliance and Scots Review* contains a letter from Eliot protesting against the reference in the previous issue to Ezra Pound as a 'self-convicted traitor'. The *Review* also prints an editorial apology.

26 September: *Life* magazine quotes about 60 lines of *The Cocktail*

Party in a report of the première of the play at the Edinburgh Festival; this is the first appearance in print of any lines of the play.

November: The small literary periodical, *Adam*, prints Eliot's 'The Aims of Poetic Drama'. Eliot discusses the 'problems of poetic drama' with particular reference to his own plays, *The Family Reunion* and *The Cocktail Party*.

19 December: *The Cocktail Party* opens for a two-week run at the Theatre Royal, Brighton. The first-night audience includes Ivor Novello, and Gilbert Miller, the New York producer.

1950

3 January: Eliot writes to Walter Turner Levy that he is leaving for a holiday in South Africa.

21 January: *The Cocktail Party* opens in New York at the Henry Miller theatre on Broadway', the audience including the Duke and Duchess of Windsor, Ethel Barrymore and Gladys Cooper. The critics are mixed in their response but there is no doubt that it will become the most talked-about play of the season. *The Journal American* calls it 'a masterpiece. . . And as modern as an atomic bomb in its method and motivation'. *The Daily Post* says: 'The greatest of living poets has been trying to storm the drama for a long time, but at last he has mastered it.' Less favourably, Brooks Atkinson of *The New York Times* declares himself 'one theatregoer who does not understand Mr. Eliot's dogma' and *The World-Telegram and Sun* calls the play 'more suited to reading than to hearing.' *Time* magazine calls it 'a major event in the theater' that 'operates at a different level from any new play that Broadway has offered in years'.

25 January: E. Martin Browne writes to Eliot that *The Cocktail Party* is 'a very big success', and will run for at least a season.

29 January: *The New York Times Magazine* prints about 145 lines of Sir Henry Harcourt-Reilly's speeches from *The Cocktail Party*, with the heading 'The Human Mind Analyzed by T. S. Eliot'.

6 March: Eliot appears on the front cover of *Time* magazine. An article inside the magazine comments on the commercial success of *The Cocktail Party*, all the more strange from 'an expatriate, obscurely highbrow poet'. The writer also comments on Eliot's importance as 'a commentator on his age', in spite of the fact that he has given up his US citizenship and 'talks like an Englishman'.

9 March: *The Cocktail Party* is published by Faber & Faber.

12 March: In a letter to Eliot congratulating him on the success of *The Cocktail Party*, Wyndham Lewis suggests that the part of Sir Henry Harcourt Reilly might be something of a self-portrait. (Rose, 1963)

3 May: *The Cocktail Party* opens in London at the New Theatre, with a new cast including Rex Harrison as Sir Henry Harcourt-Reilly and Margaret Leighton as Celia. The play runs until February 1951.

4 July: Eliot gives a lecture, 'What Dante Means to Me', at the Italian Institute in London. He talks of Dante's two main achievements: that of having left his 'own language, more highly developed, more refined, and more precise than it was before' and his 'width of emotional range'.

2 August: Eliot gives a party to celebrate the hundredth British performance of *The Cocktail Party*. It has had over 200 performances in New York, and *Variety* reports that it has grossed over $20,000 at the Henry Miller Theatre. *The New Statesman* publishes satirical verses celebrating this under the title 'Nightingale among the Sweenies'

> Author, author, take your bow,
> *Cocktail Party* is O.K. now,
>   Still it's a riddle how
>   Lowbrow and middlebrow
> Mix with the highbrow at this highbrow wow!

25 September: *The Adventures of Huckleberry Finn*, by Mark Twain, is published by the Cresset Press, London, with an introduction by Eliot in which he remembers the Mississippi landscape of his youth: 'The River gives the book its form . . . It is a treacherous and capricous dictator . . . it carries down human bodies, cattle and houses.'

October/November: Eliot visits the University of Chicago as poet in residence; and delivers four lectures, 'The Aims of Education'. Generally, Eliot discusses the 'tendency to universal standardization in education everywhere' and makes a plea that education should 'develop and cultivate the mind and sensibility' rather than having the object of earning a living. He finishes by discussing the 'problem of religion in education' and the inadequacy of the 1944 Education Act in providing the correct quantity or quality of religious training.

21 November: Eliot delivers 'Poetry and Drama', the first Theodore Spencer Memorial Lecture, at Harvard University. In it he expresses his uncertainty over *The Family Reunion*: 'I had given my attention to versification, at the expense of plot and character. . . '

2 December: Eliot remarks to Walter Turner Levy, that because of the success of *The Cocktail Party* and his having been awarded the Nobel Prize: 'No one thinks of me as a poet any more, but as a celebrity.' (Levy and Scherle, 1968).

On his return from the USA Eliot suffers a mild heart attack and is hospitalized for a short period.

20 December: A letter by Eliot on 'The Television Habit' is printed in

The Times, following a story that the BBC propose to spend over £4m on the development of television. Eliot pleads that this decision be very carefully considered: he has just returned from the USA, where television is a 'habitual form of entertainment' and where responsible Americans are increasingly concerned, not only with the quality of the programmes, but 'with the television habit, whatever the programme might be'.

24 December: *The Sunday Times* 'Books of the Year' prints Eliot's choices: *L'Amie de Madame Maigret* by Simenon; the Archbishop of York's *Church and State in England*; 'the important edition' of *Pascal's Pensées* by the late H. F. Stewart; *Religion and Culture*, 'Mr. Christopher Dawson's Gifford Lectures'; E. R. Curtius' *Europäische Litteratur und Lateinisches Mittelalter* (of which Eliot has read only 'certain chapters'); and *La Pesanteur et la Grace* by the late Simone Weil, 'almost too important to be included in one's list of reading for one year only'. In 1952 Eliot will write a preface to Simone Weil's *The Need for Roots*.

During 1950 the post of Eliot's private secretary becomes vacant and Eliot employs Valerie Fletcher, from Yorkshire, who has been Charles Morgan's private secretary. In 1957 she will become his second wife.

1951

16 June: Eliot addresses the Friends of Chichester Cathedral on 'The Value and Use of Cathedrals in England Today'. Discussing current comment on the dwindling size of congregations, Eliot makes a plea that cathedrals should not be judged by standards of mere utility: 'It is in the cathedrals that we ought to affirm the last stronghold of leisure, for the sake of scholarship and theology.'

28 June: The screenplay of Eliot's *Murder in the Cathedral* is published for the film's first showing at the International Film Festival in Venice.

September: Donald Hall, the American poet, then a young Harvard graduate student about to go to Oxford, recalls (Hall, 1978) visiting Eliot at this time:

> Eliot was only sixty-three, in the autumn of 1951, but he looked at least seventy-five . . . His face was pale as baker's bread. He stooped as he sat at his desk . . . He smoked, and between inhalations he hacked a dry, deathly, smoker's hack. His speech – while precise, exact, perfect – was slow to move, as if he stood behind the boulder of each word, pushing it into view. Eliot was *cadaverous*, in 1951.

13 September: Eliot's 'Virgil and the Christian World' is published in *The Listener*. Eliot discusses the theme that Virgil, among the classical poets and prose writers, is 'uniquely near to Christianity' both chronologically, and with regard to the content of his work.

18 November: Eliot arrives in Paris to open the exhibition 'Le Livre Anglais' organized by the Bibliothèque Nationale. John Hayward has been a consultant in the planning of the exhibition and Eliot's opening speech (Sencourt, 1971) dealing with the relation between creative writing and bibliography, is in some respects a tribute to his friendship with Hayward.

15 December: 'World Tribute to Bernard Shaw', a letter by Eliot, is published in *Time and Tide*. A fund of £250,000 is to be set up in Shaw's memory for three purposes: to assist young writers and musicians; to maintain Shaw's house at Ayot St Lawrence; and to continue the performance of Shaw's plays. Eliot is suspicious of the practicalities of any such scheme: 'We need to know how it proposed that the money should be administered, and, above all, by whom.'

1952

25 January: Joseph Pieper's *Lesiure as the Basis of Culture* is published by Faber & Faber, with an introduction by Eliot in which he regrets the modern trend to disassociate theology from philosophy; and describes Pieper as an explicitly Catholic philosopher, grounded in Plato and Aristotle, and thus an exponent of Eliot's own views.

7 March: Simone Weil's *L'Enracinement*, translated as *The Need for Roots*, is published by Routledge & Kegan Paul, with a preface by Eliot.

18 April: A film edition of *Murder in the Cathedral* is published by Faber & Faber, containing the original text of the play, with some new scenes written especially for the film by Eliot.

Contemporary French Poetry, by Joseph Chiari, a friend of Eliot's, is published by Manchester University Press, containing chapters on Valéry, Claudel, St John Perse, Eluard and the Surrealists. In his foreword Eliot comments that, in introducing important French poets to an English readership, Chiari has performed a task similar to that of Arthur Symons in his *Symbolist Movement in French Literature* (1899) (the volume in which Eliot discovered the most important influence on his early poetry, Jules Laforgue).

22 July: Eliot delivers an address to the members of the London Library, the largest private library in Britain, on the occasion of his election as President. He recalls that he first became a member in the early 1920's, when he was reviewing for *The Athenaeum* and *The Times Literary Supplement.* Because of the Library's extensive stock and the fact they allowed members to take books away, 'it was the London Library that made my literary journalism possible'.

September: *The Animals' Magazine* publishes 'Cat Morgan's Apology through the Pen of T. S. Eliot', a poem of five 4-line stanzas first published in *Faber Book News*. A note records Cat Morgan's death from extreme old age on 7 July 1952'.

20 November: Eliot's *The Complete Poems and Plays (1909–1950)* is published by Faber & Faber.

6 December: Eliot's article, 'The Publishing of Poetry', given as a talk to the Society of Young Publishers in November, is printed in *The Bookseller*. Eliot says that he speaks with the experience of 25 years of publishing poetry, and begins by commenting that poetry is the only category of publishing which is expected to lose money. He suggests there are two conditions for successful poetry publishing: the first is that a publisher must be convinced that it is his duty to add to the heritage of English poetry, and the second is that there should be someone in the publishing house with a flair for recognising which young poets will become major writers. Eliot also stresses the value of poetry journals and small independent publishers.

8 December: E. Martin Browne writes to Eliot that he has received the draft of the first two acts of *The Confidential Clerk*. Eliot has been working intermittently on this play for about a year, and it will go into several more drafts before its completion in summer 1953.

21 December: An announcement appears in the *Sunday Times* that *The Cocktail Party* has played to nearly a million and a half spectators, and that five theatres in New York have offered to put it on after its opening at the Edinburgh Festival.

1953

17 January: A letter by Eliot on Charles Maurras is printed in *Time and Tide*, following an obituary note on him in the previous issue. (Maurras died in December 1952.) Eliot says that the description of Maurras as a Catholic Royalist is misleading; that Maurras was a rationalist who supported the church on political and social grounds. Eliot also rejects the statement that Maurras was a Fascist: 'He had formulated his own political philosophy long before Fascism was ever heard of.'

Spring: Donald Hall (Hall, 1978) recalls attending a rally at the Institute of Contemporary Arts, supporting the notion that Pound should be set free from St Elizabeths Hospital. Eliot is in the chair.

March: Eliot's *Selected Prose*, edited by John Hayward, is published by Penguin Books in an edition of approximately 40,000.

9 June: Eliot delivers an address, 'American Literature and the American Language', at Washington University in St Louis; in which, recalling his boyhood in that town, he describes how he was brought up to be conscious of the 'Law of Public Service' as it operated through Church, City and University: 'I think it is a very good beginning for any child, to be brought up to reverence such institutes.' Eliot also discusses the differences in the English and American traditions of poetry, but refuses to give any definitions of an 'English' or 'American' poet because such a term could never be wholly comprehensive.

Mid-June: From St Louis Eliot goes to Cambridge, Massachusetts; where he stays with his sister-in-law, then back to New York where he stays with his publisher and friend, Robert Giroux.

29 June: Eliot meets Walter Turner Levy in New York and tells the recently ordained Levy how pleased he is that he wants to continue teaching rather than take a parish; Levy recalls him commenting on the lack of good teachers and the decline of standards in education. Eliot also talks about *The Confidential Clerk*, soon to go into rehearsal, describing it as: 'less complicated on the surface than *The Cocktail Party*, but has much more in layers to be meditated on and thought of as meanings of life.' (Levy and Scherle, 1968).

27 July: Rehearsals start in London for *The Confidential Clerk*, produced by E. Martin Browne.

25 August: *The Confidential Clerk* opens at the Lyceum Theatre, Edinburgh, as part of the Edinburgh Festival, with Paul Rogers as Sir Claude Mulhammer and Margaret Leighton as Lucasta Angel. Its plot is based on the *Ion* or Euripides, with the theme of the hidden son of a god (doubled in Eliot's version, as in *The Comedy of Errors*) and a mortal woman. The play is favourably received but not considered to be an achievement on the same level as *Murder in the Cathedral* or *The Cocktail Party*. *The Times* says: 'It is likely to be found brilliantly entertaining even by those who are left wondering what it is all really about.' Ivor Brown, writing for *The New York Herald Tribune*, calls the play 'a light artificial comedy which suggests Oscar Wilde at slightly below best form'. W. A. Darlington of *The New York Times* comments: Eliot . . . is now by common consent the most important contemporary writer for the English-speaking stage and from the point of view of technical achievement *The Confidential Clerk* is his best play. Not, let it be clearly stated, his most important play. It is a light comedy and though its undertones are deep they remain undertones.'

September: Walter Turner Levy sends the typescript of his doctoral thesis on William Barnes to Eliot, as well as the latest book by Walt Kelly, the American cartoonist whose most famous character is Pogo. Eliot will reply on 14 December.

16 September: *The Confidential Clerk* opens at the Lyric Theatre, Shaftsbury Avenue where it will run until April 1954 and then transfer to the Duke of York's for another four weeks.

Autumn: Henry Sherek assembles a cast in New York for the Broadway opening of *The Confidential Clerk*.

19 November: Eliot delivers 'The Three Voices of Poetry', the eleventh lecture of the National Book League, at Central Hall, Westminster; it will be published in December by the Cambridge University Press. In his *Diaries* (1966) Harold Nicolson recalls that the audience was over 2,500, and that Eliot talked about: 'his Three Voices – the voice of the poet talking to himself or nobody, the voice of a poet addressing the audience, and the voice of a poet speaking through a dramatic character.' Eliot discusses poetic inspiration, remembering that the commision to write *The Rock* in 1933, had the effect on him: 'that vigorous cranking sometimes has upon a motor car when the battery is run down'.

November/December: Wyndham Lewis and Eliot exchange correspondence about possible means of effecting Pound's release from St Elizabeths insane asylum. (Stock, 1970).

29 November: With *The Confidential Clerk* about to open on Broadway, Eliot is interviewed by John Lehmann in *The New York Times Book Review*. He describes his life in London and his work at Faber & Faber, and also recalls some turning points in his poetic career: how writing the 'Ariel Poems' released him from his silence after 'The Hollow Men' and led to the writing of 'Ash Wednesday'; how the starting-point of 'Burnt Norton' was 'lines and fragments that were discarded in the course of the production of *Murder in the Cathedral*'; and how 'Burnt Norton' might have remained a single poem had it not been for the outbreak of World War II, the inspiration of 'East Coker'; and how 'it was only in writing 'East Coker' that I began to see the Quartets as a set of four'.

14 December: Eliot replies to Levy's letter of September, urging him to find an American publisher for his manuscript, and thanking him for the 'Pogo Papers'. He suggests that Kelly, their author, may have been influenced by Joyce's *Finnegans Wake*; and also recalls Krazy Kat, a cartoon character popular with Eliot during his Harvard days. (Levy and Scherle, 1968).

15 December: Rehearsals for the American production of *The Confidential Clerk* begin in New York. Ina Claire is Lady Elizabeth and Claude Rains, an English actor turned Hollywood star and American citizen, is Sir Claude, with Joan Greenwood as Lucasta.

1954

January: *The Confidential Clerk* has short pre-Broadway runs in New Haven (at Yale University), Boston and Washington.

22 January: The *Literary Essays of Ezra Pound* are published by Faber & Faber, edited and with an introduction by Eliot.

February: The newly re-launched *London Magazine*, edited by John Lehmann, contains 'A Message' from Eliot, stressing the importance of small literary magazines in maintaining the vitality of the world of contemporary letters.

1 February: Life magazine publishes an article on *The Confidential Clerk* entitled 'T. S. Eliot Turns to Comedy', quoting some 47 lines from the play.

11 February: The *Confidential Clerk* opens at the Morosco Theatre, on Broadway; it will run until the summer. As with *The Cocktail Party*, New York critics are divided. The *Mirror* calls it 'superlative theatre', but the *Herald-Tribune* says: 'The play as a whole gives off a curious double image like a Sunday comic strip in which the colours have slipped.' *The New York Times* writes: 'A deliberate attempt to be ordinary. Unfortunately, Mr. Eliot has succeeded.'

21 February.   The *New York Times Magazine* prints about 150 lines from *The Confidential Clerk* under the general heading 'T. S. Eliot on Life and Its Paradoxes' with the subheadings 'On the Joys of Creation', 'On Living', 'On People', 'On Love and Marriage', and 'On the Family'.

Also in New York, *This Week* prints lines from *The Confidential Clerk* as captions to photographs of members of the cast.

5 March: *The Confidential Clerk* is published by Faber & Faber.

April.   Ezra Pound's recent translation of *The Women of Trachis* is broadcast on the BBC, following Eliot's and John Hayward's recommendations.

Eliot suffers a serious heart attack and is treated in the London Clinic. He is also increasingly troubled by bronchial weakness, and spends the winter out of England whenever possible.

28 May: *Religious Drama: Mediaeval and Modern* by Eliot is published in the USA by House of Books.

21 August: Eliot writes to Walter Turner Levy, who during the summer has been priest-in-charge of All Angels' Church in New York: 'It seems to me a very good thing to start in Low Churchmanship and to find oneself moving towards higher churchmanship. For the movement should come from the inside, I think: so that, as one's devotion and one's theological understanding grow, the outer forms will come to appear as the right form of expression.' (Levy and Scherle, 1968).

26 October: Eliot's poem *The Cultivation of Christmas Trees* is published by Faber & Faber, with illustrations by David Jones, the Welsh poet, painter and illustrator.

29 October: Eliot broadcasts on the Welsh Home Service of the BBC on David Jones's *In Parenthesis* and *The Anathemata*.

31 October: The Italian literary magazine, *Il Mare*, prints an Italian translation of a letter from Eliot, 'Clemenza per Ezra Pound' ('Mercy for Ezra Pound'). Eliot calls Pound 'the greatest living master of English poetry' and says that he remembers well a visit to Pound in Rapallo some 25 years earlier. He adds he would like to make another visit to Rapallo and to find Pound there again.

21 December: In his *Diaries* (1966) Harold Nicolson records a dinner at the Arts Council in honour of the departing French ambassador, hosted by Kenneth Clark and his wife. Guests are drawn from those prominent in a particular field, and include Eliot representing literature, the Oliviers for the theatre, Margot Fonteyn for ballet, William Walton for music and Graham Sutherland for painting.

26 December: *The Sunday Times* contains Eliot's 'Books of the Year': *Systematic Theology* by Paul Tillich, *The Heresy of Democracy* by Lord Percy of Newcastle, and *Self-Condemned*, a novel by Wyndham Lewis.

1955

5 March: *Le Figaro Litteraire* contains a tribute to Paul Claudel, the great French poet, occasioned by his death. The tribute includes contributions (in French) by W. H. Auden, Giuseppe Ungaretti and Eliot.

19 April: Eliot makes a speech on 'The Literature of Politics' at a luncheon given by the Education Advisory Committee of the London Conservative Union; it will be published in June by the Conservative Political Centre, with a foreword by Sir Anthony Eden. In this speech Eliot pays tribute to his old mentor, Charles Maurras.

5 May: Eliot receives the Hanseatic Goethe Award in Hamburg, and delivers an address 'Goethe as the Sage', generally considered one of his least satisfactory performances. Bernard Bergonzi (1972) comments: 'It is a strangely rambling and even incoherent performance, in which Eliot refers in an embarrassed and apologetic way to his own doubts and reservations about Goethe, but without ever quite withdrawing them. He proceeds with all the evasiveness and obliquity of which he was master, and with plentiful padding, largely to bypass Geothe's poetry, and to concentrate on Goethe's virtues as sage and great European figure.

Ronald Duncan recalls (1968) asking Eliot: 'Isn't it a bit of a grind for you to write about Goethe?'; to which Eliot replied: 'It is. I can't stand his stuff.'

Early summer: After his speech in Hamburg Eliot goes to the USA and among other engagements gives poetry readings in New York to the Y.M.C.A. and the Young Mens' Hebrew Association. He also pays his usual visit to Pound in St Elizabeths Hospital, Washington D.C.

27 September: An obituary letter by Eliot on Donald Brace, of Harcourt Brace & Co., his American publishers, is printed in *The Times*. Eliot pays tribute to Brace's business acumen and his loyalty to the authors he published.

1956

9 March: An article by Eliot, 'Father Cheetham retires from Gloucester Road', is published in *The Church Times*. St Stephens, Gloucester Road, is Eliot's parish church, where he has served as Vicar's Warden since 1934. Eliot pays tribute to Father Cheetham's achievement in having made the church: 'a centre of Evangelical Catholicism: truly Catholic and truly wholly Anglican'.

19 April: Eliot sails for the USA for a six-week visit.

30 April: Eliot delivers the Gideon D. Seymour lecture, 'The Frontiers of Criticism' at the University of Minnesota in Minneapolis. Generally, Eliot discusses 'the transformation of literary criticism which we may say began with Coleridge but which has proceeded with greater acceleration during the last twenty-five years', stressing the dangers both of over-exegesis and of criticism being too impressionistic. He describes his own literary criticism as a 'by-product of my private poetry-workshop; or a prolongation of the thinking that went into the formation of my own verse'. He also comments on the notes which were added to the Boni & Liveright edition of *The Waste Land* (1923), explaining that the main object in inserting them was that the volume would otherwise have been too short; and calling them 'the remarkable exposition of bogus scholarship that is still in view today'.

June: A revival of *The Family Reunion* opens at the Phoenix Theatre in London, with Sybil Thorndike and Paul Scofield, and produced by Peter Brook. *The Times* comments that Brook and Scofield. . .'are determined to show that the play has virtues far outweighing its admitted defects and in a revival as good as we can ever expect to see they go a long way towards justifying their act of faith.'

Eliot suffers an attack of tachycardia on the voyage back to England.

12 June: The United Press, under the headline 'Exhausted T. S. Eliot Rushed to Hospital' reports:

> Poet-playwright T. S. Eliot, exhausted by a six-week visit to his native United States, was taken by ambulance from the liner Queen Mary to a hospital today, suffering an abnormally rapid heartbeat. The 67-year-old Nobel Prize winner was stricken two days outside New York on the voyage back from his trip to America. He has been afflicted for some time with an abnormally rapid heart-beat, known medically as tachycardia. Ship officials said Mr. Eliot made the last half of the crossing in sick bay. When the ship reached Southampton, he was taken ashore, pale but smiling, by wheelchair and put into an ambulance. At the French Hospital in London, a spokesman said Mr. Eliot was 'much better'.

July: René Wellek, the eminent historian of criticism, makes the following statement typical of much critical commentary on Eliot, in the *Sewanee Review*:

> His influence on contemporary taste in poetry is most conspicuous: he has done more than anybody else to promote the 'shift of sensibility' away from the taste of the 'Georgians' and to revaluate the major figures and periods in the history of English poetry. He reacted most strongly against Romanticism, he criticized Milton and the Miltonic tradition, he exalted Dante, the Jacobean dramatists, the metaphysical poets, Dryden, and the French symbolists as '*the* tradition' of great poetry.

2 July: Eliot writes to Walter Turner Levy saying he has almost recovered and that he is going to see the revival of *The Family Reunion* at the Phoenix Theatre. (Levy, 1963).

19 July: A letter by Eliot on 'Kipling and the O.M.' (Order of Merit) is printed in *The Manchester Guardian*. Eliot defends Rudyard Kipling from a charge, made by a recent biographer, that Kipling resented the fact that Edward VII only offered him the O.M. late in life; pointing out that Kipling was first offered it at the age of 56. (Eliot himself received the O.M. in 1948, at the age of 59.)

August/September: Eliot spends a month's holiday in Switzerland.

Winter: Eliot's health again deteriorates and he is unable to go to his daily worship at St Stephens, going instead to the nearer Chelsea Old Church, where Thomas More had worshipped.

11 December: A letter by Eliot on Shaw's *Pygmalion* is printed in *The Times*. The musical version, *My Fair Lady*, is about to open in London and Eliot deplores an attempt by the Society of Authors to prevent any simultaneous production of Shaw's original play — according to Eliot, this should be left to the discretion of producers. Eliot says he has the advantage of having seen *My Fair Lady* in New York, and 'it should have great success in London'.

During 1956 Eliot has started to work on his final play, originally called *The Rest'Cure* but later titled *The Elder Statesman*. Based on Sophocles' last work, *Oedipus at Colonus*, it deals with themes of love and duty, and the love scenes between Charles and Monica have been seen as inspired by Eliot's own feelings for Valerie Fletcher.

1957

10 January: Eliot marries Valerie Fletcher, his secretary, at St Barnabas's Church, Addison Road, Kensington. Eliot's best man is Gordon Higginson, his solicitor, and Eliot makes the discovery that Jules Laforgue, the French Symbolist poet who influenced his early poetry, was married in the same church. After the wedding the Eliots take up residence in Kensington Court Gardens.

Eliot's second marriage creates a breach with John Hayward never to be healed; and they are only to meet on two more occasions. (Hayward's letters from Eliot and personal papers relating to him will eventually be bequeathed to King's College, Cambridge, not to be released until the year 2000.)

14 January: A letter drafted by the poet Archibald McLeish, Ezra Pound's friend, and signed by Eliot, Ernest Hemingway and Robert Frost, is sent to the Attorney General of the USA; it suggests that Pound is 'now unfit for trial' and regrets that the Department of Justice has remitted the case to the medical authorities for disposition on medical grounds.

10 March: Eliot's article, 'The Importance of Wyndham Lewis', is printed in *The Sunday Times*. (Lewis died on 7 March.) Eliot says of Lewis: 'A great intellect is gone, a great modern writer is dead.'

September: A speech by Eliot to the governors of the BBC is printed in the *London Magazine*, in which he protests against the reduction of the Third Programme (specializing in the arts), and the BBC's recent description of further education as a minority interest. Eliot is spokesman for literature on a delegation formed by the Sound Broadcasting Society to defend the quality of radio broadcasting; other delegates include Vaughan Williams and Michael Tippett for music, and Lawrence Olivier for drama.

13 September: Eliot's *On Poetry and Poets* is published by Faber & Faber, dedicated to his wife; all the essays included have been written over the previous 17 years, except for Milton I (1936) and 'Sir John Davies' (1926) which was 'rescued from oblivion' (as Eliot says in his preface) by John Hayward.

20 September: Eliot gives a 'unique photo-interview', entitled 'Stepping Out a Little? I Like the Idea', to the *Daily Express*. Under a photograph of himself and his wife looking at a copy of *On Poetry and Poets*, Eliot mentions a new play on which he has been working for two years (*The Elder Statesman*), describes his writing habits ('I usually write from ten till one') and recalls his days at Lloyds Bank ('They were eight valuable years, and I enjoyed them'). He finishes the interview by commenting on the *Daily Express*'s report, when he was photographed at a ball, that he was 'stepping out' a little more since his marriage: 'I like the idea. I am thinking of taking dancing lessons, as I have not danced at all for some years.'

1958

April: Eliot and his wife travel to the USA. They go to the University of Texas to give a poetry reading and to open an exhibition of his first editions and papers.

Ezra Pound is cleared of the charge of treason and discharged from St Elizabeths Hospital; he eventually returns to Rapallo, Italy.

12 May: Eliot opens the New University Library at the University of Sheffield.

16 June: Paul Valéry's *The Art of Poetry* is published by Pantheon Books in New York, as one of the Bollingen Series, with an introduction by Eliot.

5 July: In a letter to the painter Edward Burray, Conrad Aiken describes a recent evening with Eliot and his wife in a bar in New York. Eliot was 'in excellent form'.

25 August: *The Elder Statesman*, dedicated to Valerie Eliot, is produced at the Edinburgh Festival by E. Martin Browne, with Paul Rogers as Sir Henry Claverton, Anna Massey as Monica and Alec McGowen as Michael. The critics are respectful but not over-enthusiastic. Harold Hobson in *The Sunday Times* calls the play 'both peaceful and profound'; Christopher Salmon in 'Comment' on the Third Programme calls Lord Claverton 'one of Mr. Eliot's hollow men'; and the *Daily Express* says 'The play is subtly witty, finely phrased, if never exactly exciting. . .This is minor Eliot.' Kenneth Tynan, in *The Observer*, speaks for the younger generation: 'Towards the end, to be sure, he casts over the play a sedative, autumnal glow of considerable beauty . . . On the whole, however, the evening offers little more than the mild pleasure of hearing ancient verities tepidly restated.'

25 September: *The Elder Statesman* opens at the Cambridge Theatre, London where it will have a two-month run.

26 September: Eliot's seventieth birthday. He gives a supper party for the cast of *The Elder Statesman*; and *T. S. Eliot: A Symposium for his Seventieth Birthday*, edited by Neville Braybrooke, is presented to him.

14 October: In a postscript to *The Times* on the obituary notice of Dr Bell, Bishop of Chichester, Eliot states his 'gratitude and affection'; recalling that in 1934 Dr Bell invited him to write a play for the Canterbury Festival, which became *Murder in the Cathedral*: 'To Dr Bell's initiative. . . I owe my admission to the theatre'.

21 October: Eliot gives an address, 'The Unfading Genius of Rudyard Kipling', at the annual luncheon of the Kipling Society.

11 November: A letter to *The Times* by Eliot on 'Independent Television' is printed. As a well-known spokesman for the maintenance of broadcasting standards, Eliot fears that the spread of independent television will be yet one more factor in threatening the standards of the BBC.

16 December: Aldous Huxley, writing to Dr Humphrey Osmond, says that a recent visit to London he has seen Eliot, whom he describes as: 'now curiously dull — as a result, perhaps, of being, at last, happy in his second marriage.'

From 1958 to 1963 Eliot sits on the Commission for the Revised Psalter of Common Prayer, whose chairman is Dr Donald Coggan, later Archbishop of Canterbury. Bishop Coverdale's version of the Psalter, which predates the Authorized Version, has been retained up to this time for Anglican worship and the object of the Committee is to revise its text, eliminating obscurities and errors of translation.

1959

10 January: The Eliots spend their second wedding anniversary in Nassau.

19 March: *Katherine Mansfield and Other Literary Studies*, by J. Middleton Murry, is published by Constable, with a foreword by Eliot. Eliot remembers Murry's editorship of *The Athenaeum* and comments that: 'The three writers, essays on whom compose this book (George Gissing, Katherine Mansfield and Henry Williamson). . .are also important to us because they were important to Murry.'

10 April: *The Elder Statesman* is published by Faber & Faber.

Spring/Summer: The *Paris Review* publishes an interview with Eliot, 'The Art of Poetry', by Donald Hall, the American poet and poetry editor of the *Paris Review*. Hall comments that Eliot is looking tanned, much better than when he had seen him three years before, and begins by asking Eliot about his early work and life, for instance about his comment that Ezra Pound's verse was 'touchingly incompetent', to which Eliot replies: 'Hah! That *was* a bit brash, wasn't it?' Eliot goes on to disclaim that he was ever writing 'against anything': 'I don't think good poetry can be produced in a kind of political attempt to overthrow some existing form. I think it just supercedes.' He also talks about his most recent play, *The Elder Statesman*, and when asked about his theories of poetic drama, says he is not interested in those formulated before 1934: 'I have thought less about theories since I have given more time to writing for the theatre.' He feels that the 'Four Quartets' are his best work: 'I'd like to feel they get better as they go on'; and comments that his best critical essays are on poets who had influenced him, before he thought of writing about them. He finishes by suggesting that his poetry: 'in its sources, in its emotional springs, comes from America'.

7 May: Eliot's addition to the obituary notice of Ashley Dukes is printed in *The Times*; Eliot recalls the time when Dukes saw *Murder in the Cathedral* at Canterbury and subsequently brought it to his Mercury Theatre for a London run: 'Owing to his enterprise a play designed for a special occasion and for a very brief run came to the notice of the general public.'

Summer: The Dante Gold Medal is conferred on Eliot in Florence.

September: The opera of *Murder in the Cathedral (Assassinio nella Catedrale)*, set to music by Pizzetti, is performed in the Vatican before

John XXIII. Pope John sends Eliot a formal letter of thanks commending his services to the Christian faith.

8 October: The Eliots sail for the USA, a trip which includes visits to St Louis and Cambridge, Massachusetts. The Eliots will go to the USA every autumn up until 1963 for Eliot to give lectures and poetry readings; staying in Cambridge, Massachusetts for Christmas and visiting Eliot's sister-in-law and other old friends. On their return via New York they will usually stay with Margot Cohn, the owner of the publishing house, House of Books, on their way to a destination such as the Bahamas or the West Indies.

11 November: Eliot gives an address at the Mary Institute, St Louis, the girls' school founded by his grandfather. At the end of his address he reads 'The Dry Salvages' from the 'Four Quartets'.

8 December: Eliot writes to E. Martin Browne that he has: 'always been most desirous to see ordinary plays *written* by Christians rather than plays of *overtly* Christian purpose. In the theatre, I feel that one wants a Christian mentality to permeate the theatre, to affect it and to influence audiences who might be obdurate to plays of directly religious appeal.' (Browne, 1969).

1960

25 February: *One-Way Song*, Wyndham Lewis's book of satiric verse first published in 1933, is reprinted by Methuen, with a foreword by Eliot, in which he says that Lewis is 'one of the permanent masters of style in the English language', and suggests that his poetry has an Elizabethan quality: 'an age of writers of a vigour, opulence of diction and careless abundance which make them congenial to the genius of Lewis.'

24 July: Under the heading 'Resting', in Ephraim Hardcastle's column in the *Sunday Express*, is printed the information: 'Poet and playwright T. S. Eliot has not been well lately and has had to take a rest from his duties as director of a publishing firm. He is 71. . .Mr. Eliot. . .has very much changed his way of life (since his marriage); a "close friend" has said: "He never sees any of us now and we have completely lost touch with him." '

31 July: Eliot comments on Hardcastle's column of the previous week in a letter to the *Sunday Express*: 'no genuine friend would make such an assertion'.

18 December: In a letter to the *Observer*, Eliot condemns a 'gossipy account' of Wyndham Lewis, recently written by Edith Sitwell, and speaks of the 'warmth of sympathy and friendship' he felt for Lewis.

1961

13 January: In *The Times Literary Supplement* Eliot writes a tribute to Sir Bruce Richmond, the editor, on his ninetieth birthday. Eliot says that it was from Richmond he learned 'editorial standards'; and speaks of Richmond's 'genius as an editor'.

20 March: *A Selection of John Davidson's Poems* is published by Hutchinson, with a preface by Eliot. Eliot says of this Victorian, anti-Calvinist Scottish poet from industrial Clydeside that he is among the poets 'whose work impressed me deeply in my formative years between the ages of sixteen and twenty'. Eliot particularly remembers reading his poem 'Thirty Bob a Week', with its 'complete fitness of content and idiom: for I also had a good many dingy urban images to reveal'.

1 April: *The Times* carries an unsigned obituary notice of Sir Geoffrey Faber, by Eliot. Eliot will also give the Address at his Memorial Service. Eliot calls Faber 'A Poet Among Publishers', praising his writing (which includes a book on the Oxford Movement and *The Buried Stream*, a volume of collected poems), as well as his achievements as founder of Faber & Faber. Eliot recalls the period when he first worked for him: 'For the four years of its existence under this name (Faber & Gwyer) the business was only moderately successful'; and salutes Faber's 'courage and tenacity of purpose in his chosen profession'.

26 April: In the first letter of an occasional correspondence with Groucho Marx, Eliot writes thanking Groucho for a photo he has sent him, and promising to send one in return. (Groucho Marx, 1967).

28 April: In this and further letters to the *Times Literary Supplement* during May, Eliot comments on details of the partially published *The New English Bible*, particularly on the substitution of 'girl' for 'virgin'.

June: In a lecture at Leeds University entitled 'To Criticize the Critic', Eliot conducts a survey of his own critical career, commenting on his often-quoted preface to *For Lancelot Andrewes: Essays on Style and Order*: 'Well, my religious beliefs are unchanged, and I am strongly in favour of the maintenance of the monarchy in all countries which have a monarchy; as for Classicism and Romanticism, I find that the terms have no longer the importance to me that they once had.'

3 July: *The Times* quotes Eliot's comment that the current prosecution of D. H. Lawrence's *Lady Chatterley's Lover* is a 'deplorable blunder'. Eliot states that the book has a 'most serious and highly moral intention'.

Autumn: A production of Harold Pinter's play, *The Dumb Waiter*, opens at the Theatre Royal, Stratford, London; and Kenneth Tynan of the *Observer* compares its language and 'lurking violence' to that of Eliot's *Sweeney Agonistes*.

21 October: An article by Eliot, 'Mögen Sie Picasso?' is published in the *Frankfurter Allgemeine Zeitung* as a contribution to a symposium in honour of Picasso's eightieth birthday.

December: David Jones's poem about World War I, *In Parenthesis*, is reissued by Faber & Faber (first published by them in 1937) with an introduction by Eliot, in which he states that he was responsible for the book's first publication and that he still regards it as 'a work of genius'. He goes on to say that David Jones's work 'has some affinity with that of James Joyce (both men seem to me to have the Celtic ear for the music of words) and with the later work of Ezra Pound, and with my own'. He talks of Jones, Joyce, Pound and himself being part of 'the same literary generation' and comments: 'The lives of all of us were altered by that War, but David Jones is the only one to have fought in it.'

1962

January: An obituary note by Eliot on Harriet Weaver (owner of The Egoist Press and Eliot's first publisher) appears in *Encounter*. Eliot describes her as 'this good, kind, unassuming, courageous and lovable woman, to whom I owe so much'.

2 January: The Eliots go to Barbados for a two-month holiday.

24 March: In a letter to *The Times* (and in further letters on June 13 and August 21) Eliot continues to voice his disapproval of *The New English Bible*.

31 August: Eliot's *Collected Plays*, the first volume to contain his five major plays, is published by Faber & Faber.

4 and 14 September: In letters to *The Times* Eliot expresses agreement with Professor Dover Wilson's letter objecting to the opening of Shakespeare's tomb for purposes of scientific research; deploring the idea of disinterring a body which has been given Christian burial.

13 October: An obituary letter by Eliot on Sylvia Beach is printed in *The Times*. (See also October 1937 and July/August 1945). Eliot calls her 'a brave, generous and very lovable woman' and remembers, particularly, the financial help and encouragement she gave to James Joyce.

26 November: Eliot's *George Herbert* is published by the British Council in their series Writers and Their Work. Eliot considers Herbert a major poet, comparing the quality of his verse with that of Donne's: 'In Donne, thought seems in control of feeling, and in Herbert feeling seems in control of thought.' He describes Herbert's major work, 'The Temple', as 'a record of the spiritual struggles of a man of intellectual power and emotional intensity who gave much toil to perfecting his verses'.

December: In a questionnaire organized by the magazine *Encounter*, Eliot states that he is in favour of Britain entering the Common Market.

16 December: An article, 'T. S. Eliot on the Language of *The New English Bible*', subtitled 'Vulgar, Trivial, Pedantic. . . ' is printed in the *Sunday Telegraph*. After various textual criticisms Eliot says 'It is as much our business to attempt to arrest deterioration and combat corruption of our language, as to accept change.' He feels that, if it is generally used in churches, the new Bible will become 'an active agent of decadence'.

By the end of the year Eliot has fallen dangerously ill, and is admitted into Brompton Hospital, where he stays for five weeks.

1963

Early summer: Eliot writes to Donald Hall that he is still convalescing, but that he is spending three afternoons a week in his office. (Hall, 1978).

28 June: In a letter to *The Church Times* headed 'The "Cambridge School" and the New Morality' Eliot comments ironically on a recent lecture given by the Dean of Trinity College, Cambridge, in which the Dean condones the behaviour of a High Church Anglican seen in the bars and brothels of Tangier after a spiritual revelation. Eliot, whilst declining to comment on the current Profumo scandal and the lightness of 'popular theology and popular morals', says that if he had been an undergraduate listening to the Dean, 'I would have left at the close in a state of bewilderment.'

5 September: In an obituary letter by Eliot on Louis MacNeice in *The Times*, he speaks of 'the grief one must feel at the death of a poet of genius, younger than oneself'. Eliot, who was responsible for MacNeice's first publication by Faber & Faber, describes MacNeice as 'a poet's poet', with 'the Irishman's unfailing ear for the music of verse'.

25 September: Eliot's *Collected Poems, 1909–1962*, his final collection, is published by Faber & Faber.

October: Eliot attends the last meeting of the Commission for the Revised Psalter, held at Bishopsthorpe, the seat of the Archbishop of York, then Dr Donald Coggan. Dr Coggan later describes Eliot as: 'so frail he night have collapsed at any moment'. (Sencourt, 1971).

December: The Eliots sail for New York. They spend the winter of 1963/64 in Nassau.

1964

31 January: *Knowledge and Experience in the Philosophy of F. H. Bradley*, Eliot's doctoral dissertation of 1916, is published by the Glasgow University Press, with the dedication 'To my wife who urged me to publish this essay.' In his preface Eliot comments about his dissertation, completed 46 years before, 'I do not pretend to understand it.'

28 May: Eliot's 'Edwin Muir: An Appreciation' is published in *The Listener*. Eliot comments that it was only in the latter years of Muir's life, when he was published by Faber & Faber, that he knew Muir's work, and remembers its 'integrity'; and that Muir 'found, almost unconsciously, the right, the inevitable way of saying what he wanted to say'.

Mid-June: Groucho Marx will later describe (Groucho Marx, 1968) an enjoyable evening spent with the Eliots at their flat in London, when he discovered that he and Eliot had three things in common: 'an affection for good cigars, cats. . .and a weakness for making puns'.

14 September: Eliot is invested with the supreme civilian honour of the Medal of Freedom at the American Embassy in London, as he is too ill to travel to the USA to receive it.

Autumn: Eliot pays his last visit to his parents-in-law, in Leeds. Eliot's health is deteriorating rapidly, and he finds it difficult to go out. Father Jennings, the vicar of St Stephens, comes regularly to celebrate Holy Communion at Eliot's home.

3 December: Conrad Aiken writes to the Eliots that he is glad to hear from Valerie of Eliot's (supposed) recovery and that the doctor has told Eliot to stay at home. 'But O dear we shall miss our annual meeting in New York and the exchange of Bolos and lime rickeys at the River Club or Vanderbilt.'

1965

4 January: Eliot dies at his home in London. A few days later his body is cremated at Golders Green Crematorium.

5 January: In its obituary notice *The Times* calls Eliot 'the most influential English poet of his time'.

9 January: In an addition to Eliot's official obituary notice, 'a friend' writes in *The Times* that his friends 'will remember his spontaneous laugh. . . his enjoyment of an amusing story and the gossip of friends, . .The letter also mentions 'the radiant joy brought to his last years by his marriage'.

31 January: 'A Memoir of T. S. Eliot', by Walter Turner Levy, is printed in *The New York Times Book Review*. Levy particularly remembers his first meeting with Eliot and Eliot's encouragement of his entering the priesthood.

4 February: A memorial service for Eliot is held in Westminster Abbey. *The Times* heads its description 'Crowded Abbey laments a Poet's Passing'; *The New York Times* begins: 'The worlds of poetry and religion joined today in a memorial service for T. S. Eliot.' The Queen, the Prime Minister and President Lyndon Johnson are represented. The long list of distinguished guests includes Dame Peggy Ashcroft, Stephen Spender, Christopher Fry, the sculptor Henry Moore, and Ezra Pound, who has made the journey from Italy. The Dean of Westminster presides. Sir Alec Guinness (who played the lead in the first production of *The Cocktail Party*) reads selections from 'A Song for Simeon', 'Ash-Wednesday', 'East Coker', 'The Dry Salvages' and 'Little Gidding'. The choir sings Part iv of 'Little Gidding', set to music by Stravinsky and dedicated to Eliot. The lesson is read by Peter du Sautoy, vice-chairman of Faber and Faber, and a statement from the White House is read out: 'The President wishes to pay tribute to a poet and playwright who had a profound impact on his times and who achieved distinction on both sides of the Atlantic.'

17 February: A Requiem Mass for Eliot is held at his old parish church, St Stephen's, Gloucester Road.

17 April: An urn containing Eliot's ashes is taken to St Michael's Church, East Coker; the village from which Eliot's ancestor Andrew Eliot sailed in 1669 for New England. Above the urn a memorial bears the words: 'Of your Charity pray for the repose of the soul of Thomas Stearns Eliot, Poet.'

May: The American magazine *Atlantic* prints 'The Other T. S. Eliot' by the writer Lawrence Durrell, Lawrence's account of his friendship with Eliot as his publisher. *Encounter* also prints a 'personal memoir' by Stephen Spender.

15 July: *Selected Poems* by Edwin Muir is published by Faber & Faber in a paper-covered edition, with a preface by Eliot.

14 October: *A Memorial Volume to Aldous Huxley*, edited by Julian Huxley and published by Chatto & Windus, contains a tribute from Eliot, who recalls first glimpsing Aldous Huxley at Oxford University, during his own time as a postgraduate there (1914/15): 'The last able-bodied British undergraduates were passing from the O.T.C. (officers' training corps) to the trenches, and beyond the Rhodes scholars. . .there were hardly any left except those, who like Aldous, were wholly unfit for military service.' Eliot goes on to recall subsequently meeting Huxley at Lady Ottoline Morrell's house at Garsington.

11 November: Eliot's *To Criticize the Critic and Other Writings* is published by Faber & Faber.

Winter: The winter number of the *Sewanee Review* is a Memorial issue on Eliot.

   Sweeney Agonistes is revived in London, with a jazz accompaniment by John Dankworth.

1967

4 January: A memorial stone is placed in the floor of Westminster Abbey in Eliot's memory.

1968

26 September: A commemorative tablet to Eliot is unveiled in the Lady Chapel of St Stephen's Church, on what would have been Eliot's eightieth birthday.

1969

June: On a trip to the USA, Ezra Pound visits the New York Public Library to meet Valerie Eliot, who following the rediscovery of the original manuscript of 'The Waste Land', on which Pound had worked with Eliot, is preparing it for publication.

1971

8 November: *The Waste Land: a facsimile & transcript,* including the annotations of Ezra Pound, edited by Valerie Eliot, is published by Faber & Faber.

1972

31 August: A revival of *Murder in the Cathedral* opens at the Aldwych Theatre, London; a Royal Shakespeare Company production.

1979

18 April: A revival of *The Family Reunion* opens at the Roundhouse, London, transferring to the Vauderville.

1981

11 May: The musical *Cats*, with music by Andrew Lloyd Webber and based on Eliot's *Old Possum's Book of Practical Cats* opens at the New London Theatre, Drury Lane. Amongst enthusiastic reviews, the *Sunday Times* calls it: 'a triumphant piece of musical theatre. . .A magnificent marriage of words, music, dancing, design and direction.'

Works List

Books and Pamphlets

Prufrock and Other Observations (London: The Egoist Ltd, 1917)
[The Love Song of J. Alfred Prufrock; Portrait of a Lady; Preludes;
Rhapsody on a Windy Night; Morning at the Window; The Boston
Evening Transcript; Aunt Helen; Cousin Nancy; Mr Apollinax;
Hysteria; Conversation Galante; La Figlia Che Piange]

Ezra Pound: His Metric and Poetry (New York: Alfred A. Knopf, 1917)

Poems (London: The Hogarth Press, 1919) [Sweeney Among the Night-
ingales; The Hippopotamus; Mr Eliot's Sunday Morning Service;
Whispers of Immortality; Le Directeur; Mélange Adultère de Tout;
Lune de Miel]

Ara Vos Prec (London: The Ovid Press, 1920; New York: Alfred A.
Knopf, 1920, as *Poems*) [Burbank with a Baedeker: Bleistein with a
Cigar; Sweeney Among the Nightingales; Sweeney Erect; Mr Eliot's
Sunday Morning Service; Whispers of Immortality; The Hippopotamus;
A Cooking Egg; Lune de Miel; Dans le Restaurant; Le Directeur;
Mélange Adultère de Tout; Ode; The Love Song of J. Alfred Prufrock;
Portrait of a Lady; Preludes; Rhapsody on a Windy Night; Morning
at the Window; Conversation Galante; Aunt Helen; Cousin Nancy;
Mr Apollinax; The Boston Evening Transcript; La Figlia Che Piange]

The Sacred Wood (London: Methuen & Co. Ltd, 1920, 2/1928; New
York: Alfred A. Knopf, 1921, 2/1930) [Introduction: The Perfect
Critic; Swinburne as Critic; A Romantic Aristocrat; The Local
Flavour; A Note on the American Critic; The French Intelligence;
Tradition and the Individual Talent; The Possibility of a Poetic
Drama; Euripides and Professor Murray; 'Rhetoric' and Poetic Drama;
Some Notes on the Blank Verse of Christopher Marlowe; Hamlet and
His Problems; Ben Jonson; Philip Massinger; Swinburne as Poet;
Blake, Dante]

The Waste Land (New York: Boni and Liveright, 1922/*R* 1923; London:
The Hogarth Press, 1923; London: Faber & Faber Ltd, 1962) [The
Burial of the Dead; A Game of Chess; The Fire Sermon; Death by
Water; What the Thunder Said; Notes]

Homage to John Dryden (London: The Hogarth Press, 1924) [Preface;
John Dryden; The Metaphysical Poets; Andrew Marvell]

Poems, 1909–1925 (London: Faber & Gwyer Ltd, 1925; New York:
Harcourt, Brace and Company 1932) [Prufrock and Other Observations; Poems; The Waste Land; The Hollow Men]

Journey of the Magi (London: Faber & Gwyer Ltd, 1927; New York:
William Edwin Rudge, 1927)

Shakespeare and the Stoicism of Seneca (London: Oxford University Press, 1927) [An address read before the Shakespeare Association, 18 March 1927]

A Song for Simeon (London: Faber & Gwyer Ltd, 1928)

For Lancelot Andrewes (London: Faber & Gwyer Ltd, 1928; New York: Doubleday, Doran and Company, Inc., 1929) [Preface; Lancelot Andrewes; John Bramhall; Niccolo Machiavelli; Francis Herbert Bradley; Baudelaire in Our Time; Thomas Middleton; A Note on Richard Crashaw; The Humanism of Irving Babbit]

Dante (London: Faber & Faber Ltd, 1929)

Animula (London: Faber & Faber Ltd, 1929)

Ash-Wednesday (London: Faber & Faber Ltd, 1930; New York: G. P. Putman's Sons, 1930) [Because I do not hope to turn again; Lady, three white leopards sat under a juniper-tree; At the first turning of the second stair; Who walked between the violet and the violet; If the lost work is lost, if the spent word is spent; Although I do not hope to turn again]

Anabasis: A Poem by St. J. Perse (London: Faber & Faber Ltd, 1930, rev. 2/1959; New York: Harcourt, Brace and Company, 1938, rev. and corrected 2/1949 [A translation into English by T. S. Eliot]

Marina (London: Faber & Faber Ltd, 1930)

Thoughts after Lambeth (London: Faber & Faber Ltd., 1931)

Triumphal March (London: Faber & Faber Ltd, 1931)

Charles Whibley: A Memoir (London: Oxford University Press 1931) [An address read before the English Association, 20 February 1931]

Selected Essays, 1917–1932 (London: Faber & Faber Ltd, 1932, 2/1951; New York: Harcourt, Brace and Company, 1932, 2/1950) [Tradition and The Individual Talent; The Function of Criticism; 'Rhetoric' and Poetic Drama; A Dialogue on Dramatic Poetry; Euripides and Professor Murray; Seneca in Elizabethan Dramatists; Four Elizabethan Dramatists; Christopher Marlowe; Shakespeare and the Stoicism of Seneca; Hamlet; Ben Jonson; Thomas Middleton; Thomas Heywood; Cyril Tourneur; John Ford; Philip Massinger; Dante; The Metaphysical Poets; Andrew Marvell; John Dryden; William Blake; Swinburne as Poet; Lancelot Andrewes; John Bramhall; Thoughts after Lambeth; Baudelaire; Arnold and Pater; Francis Herbert Bradley; Marie Lloyd; Wilkie Collins and Dickens; The Humanism of Irving Babbitt; Second Thoughts about Humanism; Charles Whibley]

John Dryden: The Poet, the Dramatist, the Critic (New York: Terence & Elsa Holliday, 1932)

Sweeney Agonistes (London: Faber & Faber Ltd, 1932) [Fragment of a Prologue; Fragment of an Agon]

The Use of Poetry and the Use of Criticism (London: Faber & Faber Ltd, 1933, 2/1964; Cambridge, Massachusetts: Harvard University Press, 1933) [Prefatory Notes; Introduction; Apology for the Countess of Pembroke; The Age of Dryden; Wordsworth and

Coleridge; Shelley and Keats; Matthew Arnold; The Modern Mind; Conclusion]

After Strange Gods (London: Faber & Faber Ltd, 1934; New York: Harcourt, Brace and Company, 1934) [The Page—Barbour Lectures at the University of Virginia]

The Rock (London: Faber & Faber Ltd, 1934; New York: Harcourt, Brace and Company, 1934) [A play written for performance at Sadler's Wells Theatre, 28 May—9 June 1934]

Elizabethan Essays (London: Faber & Faber Ltd, 1934; New York: Harcourt, Brace and Company, 1956, as *Essays on Elizabethan Drama*; London: Faber & Faber Ltd, 1963, as *Elizabethan Dramatists*) [Four Elizabethan Dramatists; Christopher Marlowe; Shakespeare and the Stoicism of Seneca; Hamlet; Ben Jonson; Thomas Middleton; Thomas Heywood; Cyril Tourneur; John Ford; Philip Massinger; John Marston]

Words for Music (Bryn Mawr: Bryn Mawr Press, 1935) [New Hampshire, Virginia]

Murder in the Cathedral (London: Faber & Faber Ltd, 1935, 2/1936, 3/1937, 4/1938; New York: Harcourt, Brace and Company, 1935, 2/1936, 3/1963) [Film edition pubd in 1952 by Faber & Faber Ltd, London, and by Harcourt, Brace and Company, New York]

Two Poems (Cambridge: Cambridge University Press, 1935) [Cape Ann; Usk]

Essays Ancient and Modern (London: Faber & Faber Ltd, 1936; New York: Harcourt, Brace and Company, 1936) [Preface; Lancelot Andrewes; John Bramhall; Francis Herbert Bradley; Baudelaire in Our Time; The Humanism of Irving Babbitt; Religion and Literature; Catholicism and International Order; The *Pensées* of Pascal; Modern Education and The Classics; In Memoriam]

Collected Poems, 1909—1935 (London: Faber & Faber Ltd, 1936; New York: Harcourt, Brace and Company, 1936) [Prufrock; Poems; The Waste Land; Ash-Wednesday; Journey of the Magi; A Song for Simeon Animula; Marina; Sweeney Agonistes; Eyes that last I saw in tears; The wind sprang up at four o'clock; Five Finger Exercises; Landscapes; Lines for an Old Man; Choruses from 'The Rock']

The Family Reunion (London: Faber & Faber Ltd, 1939; New York: Harcourt, Brace and Company, 1939)

Old Possum's Book of Practical Cats (London: Faber & Faber Ltd, 1939, 2/1940 [illustrated], rev. and enlarged 3/1953; New York: Harcourt, Brace and Company, 1939/additions 1968) [Preface; The Naming of Cats; The Old Gumbie Cat; Growltiger's Last Stand; The Rum Tum Tugger; The Song of the Jellicles; Mungojerrie and Rumpelteazer; Old Deuteronomy; The Pekes and the Pollicles; Mr. Mistoffelees; Macavity: The Mystery Cat; Gus: The Theatre Cat; Bustopher Jones: The Cat about Town; Skimbleshanks: The Railway Cat; The Ad-dressing of Cats] [Later addition: Cat Morgan Introduces Himself]

The Idea of a Christian Society (London: Faber & Faber Ltd, 1939;

New York: Harcourt, Brace and Company, 1940) [Three lectures delivered at Corpus Christi College, Cambridge, March 1939]

The Waste Land and Other Poems (London: Faber & Faber Ltd, 1940; New York: Harcourt, Brace and Company, 1955) [The Love Song of J. Alfred Prufrock; Preludes; Gerontion; Sweeney among the Nightingales; The Waste Land; Ash-Wednesday; Journey of the Magi; Marina Landscapes; Two Choruses from 'The Rock']

East Coker (London: Faber & Faber Ltd, 1940)

Burnt Norton (London: Faber & Faber Ltd, 1941)

Points of View (London: Faber & Faber Ltd, 1941)

The Dry Salvages (London: Faber & Faber Ltd, 1941)

The Classics and the Man of Letters (London: Oxford University Press, 1942) [The Presidential Address delivered to the Classical Association, 15 April 1942]

The Music of Poetry (Glasgow: Jackson, Son & Company, 1942) [The W. P. Ker Memorial Lecture delivered at the University of Glasgow, 24 February 1942]

Little Gidding (London: Faber & Faber Ltd, 1942)

Four Quartets (New York: Harcourt, Brace and Company, 1943; London: Faber & Faber Ltd, 1944) [Burnt Norton; East Coker; The Dry Salvages; Little Gidding]

Reunion by Destruction (London: The Council for the Defence of Church Principles, 1943)

What is a Classic? (London: Faber & Faber Ltd, 1945) [An address delivered before the Virgil Society, 16 October 1944]

Die Einheit der Europäischen Kultur (Berlin: Carl Habel Verlagsbuch-Handlung, 1946) [Reprinted in English as an appendix to *Notes Towards the Definition of Culture*, 1948]

On Poetry (Concord, Massachusetts: Concord Academy, 1947)

Milton (London: Geoffrey Cumberlege, 1947) [Annual Lecture on a Master Mind, Henriette Hertz Trust, 26 March 1947] [Reprinted as 'Milton II' in *On Poetry and Poets*, 1957]

Selected Poems (Middlesex: Harmondsworth, 1948; New York: Harcourt, Brace & World, Inc., 1967) [The Love Song of J. Alfred Prufrock; Portrait of a Lady; Preludes; Rhapsody on a Windy Night; Gerontion; Burbank with a Baedeker: Bleistein with a Cigar; Sweeney Erect; A Cooking Egg; The Hippopotamus; Whispers of Immortality; Mr Eliot's Sunday Morning Service; Sweeney among the Nightingales; The Waste Land; The Hollow Men; Ash-Wednesday; Journey of the Magi; A Song for Simeon; Animula; Marina; Choruses from 'The Rock']

Notes towards the Definition of Culture (London: Faber & Faber Ltd, 1948, 2/1062; New York: Harcourt, Brace and Company, 1949) [Preface, Introduction, The Three Senses of 'Culture'; The Class and the Elite; Unity and Diversity; The Region; Unity and Diversity: Sect and Cult; A Note on Culture and Politics; Notes on Education and Culture: and Conclusion; Appendix: The Unity of European Culture]

From Poe to Valéry (New York: Harcourt, Brace and Company, 1948) [A lecture delivered at the Library of Congress, 19 November 1948]

The Aims of Poetic Drama (London: The Poets' Theatre Guild, 1949)

The Cocktail Party (London: Faber & Faber Ltd, 1950; New York: Harcourt, Brace and Company, 1950)

Poems Written in Early Youth (London: Faber & Faber Ltd, 1950, 2/1967; New York: Farrar, Straus and Giroux, 1967) [Introduction; A Fable for Feasters; If Time and Space, as Sages say; When We came Home across the Hill; Before Morning; Circe's Palace; On a Portrait; The moonflower opens to the moth; Nocturne; Humouresque; Spleen; Ode; The Death of Saint Narcissus; Notes]

Poetry and Drama (Cambridge, Massachusetts: Harvard University Press, 1951; London: Faber & Faber Ltd, 1951) [The Theodore Spencer Memorial Lecture, delivered at Harvard University, 21 November 1950]

The Value and Use of Cathedrals in England Today (Chichester: Friends of Chichester Cathedral, 1952) [An address delivered to the Friends of Chichester Cathedral, 16 July 1952]

An Address to Members of the London Library (London: The London Library, 1952; Providence, Rhode Island: The Providence Athenaeum, 1953) [A Presidential Address delivered to the Members of the London Library, 22 July 1952]

The Complete Poems and Plays, 1909–1950 (New York: Harcourt, Brace and Company, 1952) [Prufrock; Poems; The Waste Land; Ash-Wednesday; Journey of the Magi; A Song for Simeon; Animula; Marina; Sweeney Agonistes; Eyes that last I saw in tears; The wind sprang up at four o'clock; Five Finger Exercises; Landscapes; Lines for an Old Man; Choruses from 'The Rock'; Four Quartets; Old Possum's Book of Practical Cats; Murder in the Cathedral; The Family Reunion; The Cocktail Party]

Selected Prose (London: Penguin Books, 1953)/R 1953; R 1958) [Introduction; Literary Criticism; Social Criticism; Includes first publication in book form of 'Reflections on vers libre'; 'Virgil and Destiny'; 'Dante'; 'Yeats'; 'A Valedictorian']

American Literature and the American Language (St Louis, Missouri: Washington University, 1953) [An address delivered at Washington University, 9 June 1953] [American Literature and the American Language; The Eliot Family and St. Louis]

The Three Voices of Poetry (Cambridge: Cambridge University Press, 1953; New York: Cambridge University Press, 1954) [The 11th Annual Lecture of the National Book League, delivered 19 November 1953]

The Confidential Clerk (London: Faber & Faber Ltd, 1954; New York: Harcourt, Brace and Company, 1954)

Religious Drama: Mediaeval and Modern (New York: House of Books, Ltd, 1954) [An address delivered to the Friends of Rochester Cathedral, 1937]

The Cultivation of Christmas Trees (London: Faber & Faber Ltd,

1954; New York: Farrar, Straus and Cudahy, 1956)

The Literature of Politics (London: Conservative Political Centre, 1955) [A lecture delivered at the Overseas League, London, 19 April 1955]

The Frontiers of Criticism (Minneapolis: University of Minnesota Press, 1956) [A lecture delivered at the University of Minnesota, 13 August 1956]

On Poetry and Poets (London: Faber & Faber Ltd, 1957; New York: Farrar, Straus and Cudahy, 1957) [The Social Function of Poetry; The Music of Poetry; What is Minor Poetry?; What Is a Classic?; Poetry and Drama; The Three Voices of Poetry; The Frontiers of Criticism; Virgil and the Christian World; Sir John Davies; Milton I; Milton II; Johnson as Critic and Poet; Byron; Goethe as the Sage; Rudyard Kipling; Yeats]

The Elder Statesman (London: Faber & Faber Ltd, 1959; New York: Farrar, Straus and Cudahy, 1959)

Collected Plays (London: Faber & Faber Ltd, 1962) [Murder in the Cathedral; The Family Reunion; The Cocktail Party; The Confidential Clerk; The Elder Statesman]

George Herbert (London: The British Council, 1962; Lincoln, Nebraska: University of Nebraska Press, 1964)

Collected Poems, 1909–1962 (London: Faber & Faber Ltd, 1963; New York: Harcourt, Brace & World, Inc., 1963) [Prufrock; Poems; The Waste Land; The Hollow Men; Ash-Wednesday; Journey of the Magi; A Song for Simeon; Animula; Marina; Sweeney Agonistes; Eyes that last I saw in tears; The wind sprang up at four o'clock; Five Finger Exercises; Landscapes; Lines for an Old Man; Choruses from 'The Rock'; Burnt Norton; East Coker; The Dry Salvages; Little Gidding; Defence of the Islands; A Note on War Poetry; To the Indians Who Died in Africa; To Walter de la Mare; A Dedication to My Wife]

Knowledge and Experience in the Philosophy of F. H. Bradley (Glasgow: University Press, 1964; New York: Farrar, Straus and Company, 1964) [A dissertation submitted in 1916 for the degree of Doctor of Philosophy at Harvard University]

To Criticize the Critic and Other Writings (London: Faber & Faber Ltd, 1965; New York: Farrar, Straus and Giroux, 1965/R 1967) [To Criticize The Critic; From Poe to Valéry; American Literature and the American Language; The Aims of Education; What Dante Means to Me; The Literature of Politics; The Classics and the Man of Letters; Ezra Pound: His Metric and Poetry; Reflections on 'Vers Libre']

Contributions to Periodicals

'A Fable for Feasters', *Smith Academy Record*, viii/2 (Feb 1905), 1

'A Tale of a Whale', *Smith Academy Record*, viii/4 (April 1905), 1

'A Lyric' ('If Space and Time, as sages say'), *Smith Academy Record*, viii/4 (April 1905), 3

'The Man Who was King', *Smith Academy Record*, viii/6 (June 1905), 1

'When We came Home across the Hill', *Harvard Advocate*, lxxxiii/6 (24 May 1907), 93

'Before Morning', *Harvard Advocate*, lxxxvi/4 (13 Nov 1908), 53

'Circe's Palace', *Harvard Advocate*, lxxxvi/5 (25 Nov 1908), 66

'The Moonflower opens to the Moth', *Harvard Advocate*, lxxxvi/9 (26 Jan 1909), 130

'On a Portrait', *Harvard Advocate*, lxxxvi/9 (26 Jan 1909), 135

[A review of] *The Wine of Puritans* [By Van Wyck Brooks], *Harvard Advocate*, lxxxvii/5 (7 May 1909), 80

'The Point of View', *Harvard Advocate*, lxxxvii/6 (20 May 1909), 82 [unsigned]

'Gentlemen and Seamen', *Harvard Advocate*, lxxxvii/7 (25 May 1909), 115

[A review of] *Egoists* [By James Huneker], *Harvard Advocate*, lxxxviii/1 (5 Oct 1909), 16

'Nocturne', *Harvard Advocate*, lxxxviii/3 (12 Nov 1909), 39

'Humouresque (After J. Laforgue)', *Harvard Advocate*, lxxxviii/7 (12 Jan 1910), 103

'Spleen', *Harvard Advocate*, lxxxviii/8 (26 Jan 1910), 114

'Class Ode', *Harvard Advocate*, lxxxix/8 (24 June 1910), 100 [Reprinted on the same day in the Boston *Evening Transcript* and the Boston *Evening Herald*]

'The Love Song of J. Alfred Prufrock', *Poetry*, vi/3 (June 1915), 130

'Poems', *Blast*, 2 (July 1915), 48 [Preludes; Rhapsody on a Windy Night]

'Portrait of a Lady', *Others*, i/3 (Sept 1915), 35

'Three Poems', *Poetry*, vii/1 (Oct 1915), 21 [The Boston Evening Transcript; Aunt Helen; Cousin Nancy]

[A review of] *Theism and Humanism* [By the Rt. Hon. A. J. Balfour], *International Journal of Ethics*, xxvi/2 (Jan 1916), 284

[A review of] *The Philosophy of Nietzsche* [By A. Wolf], *International Journal of Ethics*, xxvi/3 (April 1916), 426

'Thomas Hardy', *Manchester Guardian*, 803 (23 June 1916), 3 [A review of *Thomas Hardy: A Study of the Wessex Novels*, by H. C. Duffin]

'An American Critic', *New Statesman*, vii/168 (24 June 1916), 284 [A review of *Aristocracy and Justice*, by Paul E. More; Unsigned]

[A review of] *The French Renascence* [By Charles Sarolea], *New Statesman*, vii/169 (1 July 1916), 309. [Unsigned]

'Mr. Doughty's Epic', *Manchester Guardian*, 829 (24 July 1916), 3 [A review of *The Titans*, by Charles M. Doughty]

'Mr. Leacock Serious', *New Statesman*, vii/173 (29 July 1916), 404

Works List

[A review of *Essays and Literary Studies*, by Stephen Leacock; Unsigned]

[A review of] *Social Adaptation* [By L. M. Bristol], *New Statesman*, vii/173 (29 July 1916), 405 [Unsigned]

'Observations', *Poetry*, viii/6 (Sept 1916), 292 [Conversation Galante; La Figlia Che Piange; Mr. Appolinax; Morning at the Window]

[A review of] *Conscience and Christ: Six Lectures on Christian Ethics* [By Hastings Rashdall], *International Journal of Ethics*, xxvii/1 (Oct 1916), 111

[A review of] *Group Theories of Religion and the Religion of the Individual* [By Clement C. J. Webb], *International Journal of Ethics*, xxvii/1 (Oct 1916), 115

[A review of] *Religion and Science; A Philosophical Essay* [By John Theodore Merz], *International Journal of Ethics*, xxvii/1 (Oct 1916), 125

[A review of] *The Ultimate Belief* [By A. Clutton Brock], *International Journal of Ethics*, xxvii/1 (Oct 1916), 127

[A review of] *Philosophy and War* [By Emile Boutroux], *International Journal of Ethics*, xxvii/1 (Oct 1916), 128

'The Development of Leibniz's Monadism', *Monist*, xxvi/4 (Oct 1916), 534

'Leibniz's Monads and Bradley's Finite Centers', *Monist*, xxvi/4 (Oct 1916), 566

'Charles Péguy', *New Statesman*, viii/183 (7 Oct 1916), 19 (A review of *Avec Charles Péguy, de la Lorraine à la Marne*, by Victor Boudon; Unsigned]

'Mr. Lee Masters', *Manchester Guardian*, 906 (9 Oct 1916), 3 [A review of *Songs and Satires* by Edgar Lee Masters]

'Giordano Bruno', *New Statesman*, viii/185 (21 Oct 1916), 68 [A review of *Giordano Bruno: His Life, Thought, and Martydrom*, by William Boulting; Unsigned]

[A review of] *With Americans of Past and Present Days* [By J. J. Jusserand], *New Statesman*, viii/188 (11 Nov 1916), 141 [Unsigned]

[A review of] *Elements of Folk Psychology: Outlines of a Psychological History of the Development of Mankind* [By Wilhelm Wundt], *International Journal of Ethics*, xxvii/2 (Jan 1917), 252

'Reflectors on *vers libre*', *New Statesman*, viii/204 (3 March 1917), 518 [Reprinted in *Selected Prose*, 1953]

'Diderot', *New Statesman*, viii/206 (17 March 1917), 572 [A review of *Diderot's Early Philosophical Works*, translated and ed. by Margaret Jourdain; Unsigned]

[A review of] *Union Portraits* [By Gamaliel Bradford], *New Statesman*, ix/211 (21 April 1917), 69 [Unsigned]

'Eeldrop and Appleplex', *Little Review*, iv/1 (May 1917), 7

'President Wilson', *New Statesman*, ix/214 (12 May 1917), 140 [A review of *President Wilson: His Problems and His Policy*, by H. Wilson Harris; Unsigned]

'The Borderline of Prose', *New Statesman*, ix/215 (19 May 1917), 157

'The Letters of J. B. Yeats', *Egoist*, iv/6 (July 1917), 89 [A review of *Passages from the Letters of John Butler Yeats, Selected by Ezra Pound*]

[A review of] *Mens Creatrix* [By William Temple], *International Journal of Ethics*, xxvii/4 (July 1917), 542

[A review of] *Religion and Philosophy* [By R. G. Collingwood], *International Journal of Ethics*, xxvii/4 (July 1917), 543

'Poems', *Little Review*, iv/3 (July 1917), 8 [Le Directeur; Mélange Adultère de Tout; Lune de Miel; The Hippopotamus]
Noh, or Accomplishment, a Study of the Classical Stage of Japan, by Ernest Fenollosa and Ezra Pound]

'M. Bourget's Last Novel', *New Statesman*, ix/229 (25 Aug 1917), 500 [A review of *Lazarine*, by Paul Bourget; Unsigned]

'Reflections on Contemporary Poetry, I', *Egoist*, iv/8 (Sept 1917), 118 [A review of *Strange Meetings*, by Harold Monro]

'Eeldrop and Appleplex II', *Little Review*, iv/5 (Sept 1917), 16

'A Forgotten Utopia', *New Statesman*, ix/230 (1 Sept 1917), 523 [A review of *Christianopolis: An Ideal State of the Seventeenth Century*, translated by Felix E. Held; Unsigned]

'William James on Immortality', *New Statesman*, ix/231 (8 Sept 1917), 547

[A review of] *A Defence of Idealism* [By May Sinclair], *New Statesman*, ix/233 (22 Sept 1917), 596 [Unsigned]

'Reflections on Contemporary Poetry, II', *Egoist*, iv/9 (Oct 1917), 133 [A review of *John Davidson*, by Hayim Fineman]

[A review of] *A Manual of Modern Scholastic Philosophy* [By Cardinal Mercier], *Internatonal Journal of Ethics*, xxviii/1 (Oct 1917), 137

'Reflections on Contemporary Poetry, III', *Egoist*, iv/10 (Nov 1917), 151 [A review of *The New Poetry*, ed. by Harriet Monroe and Alice C. Henderson]

'Correspondence', *Egoist*, iv/11 (Dec 1917), 165

'Turgenev', *Egoist*, iv/11 (Dec 1917), 167 [A review of *Turgenev*, by Edward Garnett]

'Short Reviews', *Egoist*, iv/11 (Dec 1917), 172 [A review of *Poems*, by Alan Seeger; *Covent Garden, and Others*, by Guy Rawlence; *Earth of Cualann*, by Joseph Campbell; *The Tenth Muse*, by Edward Thomas; Unsigned]

'A Contemporary Thomist', *New Statesman*, x/247 (29 Dec 1917), 312 [A review of *Epistemology*, by P. Coffey; Unsigned]

'In Memory of Henry James', *Egoist*, v/1 (Jan 1918), 1 [Reprinted as 'In Memory', *Little Review*, v/4 (Aug 1918), 44]

'Short Reviews', *Egoist*, v/1 (Jan 1918), 10 [A review of *The Fortune*, by Douglas Goldring; *Summer*, by Edith Wharton; Unsigned]

'Recent British Periodical Literature in Ethics', *International Journal of Ethics*, xxviii/2 (Jan 1918), 270

'Literature and the American Courts', *Egoist*, v/3 (March 1918), 39

'Verse Pleasant and Unpleasant', *Egoist*, v/3 (March 1918), 43 [A review of *Georgian Poetry, 1916–1917*, ed. by E. Marsh; *Wheels, A Second Cycle*; Signed with the pseudonym 'Apteryx']

'A Victorian Sculptor', *New Statesman*, x/256 (2 March 1918), 528 [A review of *Thomas Woolner, R. A. His Life in Letters*, by Amy Woolner; Unsigned]

'Style and Thought', *Nation*, xxii/25 (23 March 1918), 768 [A review of *Mysticism and Logic*, by Bertrand Russell; Unsigned]

'Disjecta membra', *Egoist*, v/4 (April 1918) 55 [A review of *Tendencies in Modern American Poetry*, by Amy Lowell]

'Professional, or . . . ', *Egoist*, v/4 (April 1918) 61 [A review of *The Stucco House*, by Gilbert Cannan; *Hearts of Controversy*, by Alice Meynell; Signed with the pseudonym 'Apteryx']

[A review of] *La guerra eterna e il dramma del esistenza* [By Antonio Aliotta], *International Journal of Ethics*, xxviii/3 (April 1918), 444

[A review of] *Brahmadarsanam, or Intuition of the Absolute: Being an Introduction to the Study of Hindu Philosophy* [by Sri Ananda Acharya], *International Journal of Ethics*, xxviii/3 (April 1918), 445

'Observations', *Egoist*, v/5 (May 1918), 69 [Signed with the pseudonym 'T. S. Apteryx']

'Short Notices', *Egoist*, v/5 (May 1918), 75 [A review of *On Heaven and Other Poems*, by Ford Madox Hueffer; *Dunch*, by Susan Miles; *Exiles of the Snow and Other Poems*, by Lancelot Hogben; *The Sayings of the Children*, by Pamela Glenconner; Unsigned]

'Contemporanea', *Egoist*, v/6 (June/July 1918), 84 (A review of *Tarr*, by Wyndham Lewis, *The People's Palace*, by Sacheverell Sitwell]

'Shorter Notices', *Egoist*, v/6 (June/July 1918), 87 [A review of *Chamber Music*, by James Joyce; *Potboilers*, by Clive Bell; *Resentment*, by Alec Waugh; *The Little School*, by T. Sturge Moore; *Per amica silentia lunae*, by William Butler Yeats; Unsigned]

[A review of] *The World as Imagination* [By Edward Douglas Fawcett], *International Journal of Ethics*, xxviii/4 (July 1918), 572

'New Philosophers', *New Statesman*, xi/275 (13 July 1918), 296 [A review of *Elements of Constructive Philosophy*, by J. S. Mackenzie; *The Self and Nature*, by De Witt H. Parker; *Locke's Theory of Knowledge*, by James Gibson; Unsigned]

'Short Notices', *Egoist*, v/7 (Aug 1918), 99 [A review of *In the Valley of Vision, Poems*, by Geoffrey Faber; *Sonnetts and Poems*, by Eleanor Farjeon; – *Esques*, by E. F. A. Geach and D. E. A. Wallace; *Resentment, Poems*, by Alec Waugh

'The Hawthorne Aspect of Henry James', *Little Review*, v/4 (Aug 1918), 47

'Tarr', *Egoist*, v/8 (Sept 1918), 105 [A review of *Tarr*, by Wyndham Lewis]

'Four Poems', *Little Review*, v/5 (Sept 1918), 10 [Sweeney Among the Nightingales; Whispers of Immortality; Dans le Restaurant; Mr Eliot's Sunday Morning Service]

'Studies in Contemporary Criticism, I', *Egoist*, v/9 (Oct 1918), 111

'Studies in Contemporary Criticism, II', *Egoist*, v/10 (Nov/Dec 1918), 131

'The New Elizabethans and the Old', *Athenaeum* 4640 (4 April 1919), 134 [A review of *The New Elizabethans: A First Selection of the Lives of Young Men Who Have Fallen in the Great War*, by E. B. Osborn; Unsigned]

'The Post-Georgians', *Athenaeum*, 4641 (11 April 1919), 171 [A review of *Wheels: A Third Cycle*; Unsigned]

'American Literature', *Athenaeum*, 4643 (25 April 1919), 236 [A review of *A History of American Literature, Volume 2*, ed. by William P. Trent, John Erskine, Stuart P. Sherman, Carl Van Doren]

'A Cooking Egg', *Coterie*, i (May 1919), 44

'A Romantic Patrician', *Athenaeum*, 4644 (2 May 1919), 265 [A review of *Essays in Romantic Literature*, by George Wyndham, ed. by Charles Whibley]

'Kipling Redivivus', *Athenaeum*, 4645 (9 May 1919), 297 [A review of *The Years Between*, by Rudyard Kipling]

'A Sceptical Patrician', *Athenaeum*, 4647 (23 May 1919), 361 [A review of *The Education of Henry Adams: An Autobiography*]

'Beyle and Balzac', *Athenaeum*, 4648 (30 May 1919), 392 [A review of *A History of the French Novel, to the Close of the Nineteenth Century*, by George Saintsbury]

'Two Poems', *Art and Letters*, ii/3 (Summer 1919), 103 [Burbank with a Baedeker: Bleistein with a Cigar; Sweeney Erect]

'Criticism in England', *Athenaeum*, 4650 (13 June 1919), 456 [A review of *Old and New Masters*, by Robert Lynd]

'The Education of Taste', *Athenaeum*, 4652 (27 June 1919), 520 [A review of *English Literature during the Last Half-Century*, by J. W. Cunliffe]

'Reflections on Contemporary Poetry, IV', *Egoist*, vi/3 (July 1919), 39 [A review of *Naked Warriors*, by Herbert Read; *The Charnel Rose and Other Poems*, by Conrad Aiken]

'A Foreign Mind', *Athenaeum*, 4653 (4 July 1919), 552 [A review of *The Cutting of an Agate*, by W. B. Yeats]

'The Romantic Generation, If It Existed', *Athenaeum*, 4655 (18 July 1919), 616 [A review of *Currents and Eddies in the English Romantic Generation*, by Frederick E. Pierce]

'Whether Rostand Had Something about Him', *Athenaeum*, 4656 (25 July 1919), 665 [A review of *Le Vol de la Marseillaise*, by Edmund Rostand; Rev. and reprinted as ' "Rhetoric" and Poetic Drama' in The Sacred Wood, 1920]

'Was There a Scottish Literature?', *Athenaeum*, 4657 (1 Aug 1919), 680 [A review of *Scottish Literature: Character and Influence*, by G. Gregory Smith]

'Tradition and Individual Talent, I', *Egoist*, vi/4 (Sept 1919), 54 [Reprinted in *The Sacred Wood*, 1920]

'Swinburne and the Elizabethans', *Athenaeum*, 4664 (19 Sept 1919), 909 [A review of *Contemporaries of Shakespeare*, by A. C. Swinburne, ed. by Edmund Gosse and T. J. Wise; Reprinted as 'Swinburne as Critic' in *The Sacred Wood*, 1920]

'Hamlet and His Problems', *Athenaeum*, 4665 (26 Sept 1919), 940 [A review of *The Problem of 'Hamlet'*, by the Rt. Hon. J. M. Robertson; Reprinted as 'Hamlet' in *The Sacred Wood*, 1920]

'Murmuring of Innumerable Bees', *Athenaeum*, 4666 (3 Oct 1919), 972 [A review of *Coterie: An Illustrated Quarterly*; Unsigned]

'Humanist, Artist, and Scientist', *Athenaeum*, 4667 (10 Oct 1919), 1014 [A review of *La pensée italienne au XVIme siècle et le courant libertin*, by J. Roger Charbonnel; *L'éthique de Giordano Bruno et le deuxième dialogue du Spaccio, traduction avec notes et commentaire*, by J. Roger Charbonnel]

'War-paint and Feathers', *Athenaeum*, 4668 (17 Oct 1919), 1036 [A review of *The Path of the Rainbow: An Anthology of Songs and Chants from the Indians of North America*, ed. by G. W. Cronyn]

'The Method of Mr. Pound', *Athenaeum*, 4669 (24 Oct 1919), 1065 [A review of *Quia Pauper Amavi*, by Ezra Pound]

'Tradition and the Individual Talent, II', *Egoist*, vi/5 (Nov/Dec 1919), 72 [Reprinted in *The Sacred Wood*, 1920]

'Mr Pound and His Poetry', *Athenaeum*, 4671 (7 Nov 1919), 1163 [A reply to a letter from Ezra Pound, *Athenaeum*, 31 Oct 1919]

'Ben Jonson', *Times Literary Supplement*, 930 (13 Nov 1919), 637 [A review of *Ben Jonson*, by G. Gregory Smith; Unsigned; Reprinted in *The Sacred Wood*, 1920]

'The Comedy of Humours', *Athenaeum*, 4672 (14 Nov 1919), 1180 [A review of Ben Jonson, by G. Gregory Smith, *Ben Jonson's Every Man in His Humour*, ed. by Percy Simpson]

'The Preacher as Artist', *Athenaeum*, 4674 (28 Nov 1919), 1252 [A review of *Donne's Sermons: Selected Passages*]

'The Local Flavour', *Athenaeum*, 4676 (12 Dec 1919), 1332 [A review of *Literary Studies*, by Charles Whibley; Reprinted in *The Sacred Wood*, 1920]

'Swinburne', *Athenaeum*, 4681 (16 Jan 1920), 72 [A review of *Selections from Swinburne*, ed. by Edmund Gosse and Thomas James Wise; Reprinted as 'Swinburne as Poet' in *The Sacred Wood*, 1920]

'The Naked Man', *Athenaeum*, 4685 (13 Feb 1920), 208 [A review of *William Blake the Man*, by Charles Gardner; Reprinted as 'William Blake' in *The Sacred Wood*, 1920]

'A Brief Treatise on the Criticism of Poetry', *Chapbook*, ii/9 (March 1920), 1

'Dante as a Spiritual Leader', *Athenaeum*, 4692 (2 April 1920), 441 [A review of *Dante*, by Henry Dwight Sidgwick; Reprinted as 'Dante' in *The Sacred Wood*, 1920]

'The Poetic Drama', *Athenaeum*, 4698 (14 May 1920), 635 [A review of *Cinnamon and Angelica: A Play*, by John M. Murry]

'Philip Massinger', *Times Literary Supplement*, 958 (27 May 1920),

325 [A review of *Philip Massinger*, by A. H. Cruickshank; Unsigned; Reprinted as Part 1 of 'Philip Massinger' in *The Sacred Wood*, 1920]

'The Old Comedy', *Athenaeum*, 4702 (11 June 1920), 760 [A review of *Philip Massinger*, by A. H. Cruickshank; Reprinted as Part 2 of 'Philip Massinger' in *The Sacred Wood*, 1920]

'The Perfect Critic, I', *Athenaeum*, 4706 (9 July 1920), 40 [A review of *Studies in Elizabethan Drama*, by Arthur Symons; Reprinted in *The Sacred Wood*, 1920]

'The Perfect Critic, II', *Athenaeum*, 4708 (23 July 1920), 102 [Reprinted in *The Sacred Wood*, 1920]

'The Possibility of a Poetic Drama', *Dial*, lxix/5 (Nov 1920), 441 [Reprinted in *The Sacred Wood*, 1920]

'The Second-Order Mind ', *Dial*, lxix/6 (Dec 1920), 586 [A reprint of introduction to *The Sacred Wood*]

'Notes on Current Letters', *Tyro*, 1 (Spring 1921), 4 [The Romantic Englishman; The Comic Spirit; The Function of Criticism – The Lesson of Baudelaire]

'Song to the Opherian', *Tyro*, 1 (Spring 1921), 6 [Signed with the pseudonym 'Gus Krutzsch'; Reprinted as part of 'The Wind sprang up at Four O'clock]

'Andrew Marvell', *Times Literary Supplement*, 1002 (31 Mar 1921), 201 [Unsigned, Reprinted in *Homage to John Dryden*, 1924]

'Prose and Verse', *Chapbook*, 22 (April 1921), 3

'London Letter', *Dial*, lxx/4 (April 1921), 448

'London Letter', *Dial*, lxx/6 (June 1921), 686

'John Dryden', *Times Literary Supplement*, 1012 (9 June 1921), 361 [A review of *John Dryden*, by Mark Van Doren; Unsigned; Reprinted in *Homage to John Dryden*, 1924]

'London Letter', *Dial*, lxxi/2 (Aug 1921), 213

'London Letter', *Dial*, lxxi/4 (Oct 1921), 452

'The Metaphysical Poets', *Times Literary Supplement*, 103 (20 Oct 1921), 669 [A review of *Metaphysical Lyrics and Poems of the Seventeenth Century: Donne to Butler*, ed. by Herbert J. C. Grierson; Unsigned; Reprinted in *Homage to John Dryden*, 1924]

'The Three Provincialities', *Tyro*, 2 (Spring 1922), 11 [Reprinted in *Essays in Criticism*, i/1 (Jan 1951), 38]

'London Letter', *Dial*, lxxii/5 (May 1922), 510

'Lettre d'Angleterre', *Nouvelle Revue Française*, xviii/104 (1 May 1922), 617

'Answers to the Three Questions', *Chapbook*, 27 (July 1922), 8 [A reply to a questionnaire]

'London Letter', *Dial*, lxxiii/1 (July 1922), 94

'London Letter', *Dial*, lxxiii/3 (Sept 1922), 329

'The Waste Land', *Criterion*, i/1 (Oct 1922), 50 [Reprinted in *Dial*, lxxiii/5 (Nov 1922), 473]

'London Letter', *Dial*, lxxiii/6 (Dec 1922), 659 [Reprinted as 'In Memoriam: Marie Lloyd' in *Criterion*, i/2 (Jan 1923), 192; Reprinted as 'Marie Lloyd' in *Selected Essays, 1917–1932*, 1932]

Works List

'Lettre d'Angleterre: Le style dans la prose anglaise contemporaine',
Nouvelle Revue Française, xix/111 (1 Dec 1922), 751

'Dramatis Personae', *Criterion*, i/3 (April 1923), 303

'John Donne', *Nation & Athenaeum*, xxxiii/10 (9 June 1923), 331 [A
review of *Love Poems of John Donne*]

'The Function of a Literary Review', *Criterion*, i/4 (July 1923), 421

'Andrew Marvell', *Nation & Athenaeum*, xxxiii/26 (29 Sept 1923), 809
[A review of *Miscellaneous Poems*, by Andrew Marvell]

'The Function of Criticism', *Criterion*, ii/5 (Oct 1923), 31 [Reprinted
in *Selected Essays, 1917–1932*, 1932]

'The Classics in France – and in England', *Criterion*, ii/5 (Oct 1923), 104

'The Beating of a Drum', *Nation & Athenaeum*, xxxiv/1 (6 Oct 1923),
11 [A review of *Studies in the Development of the Fool in the
Elizabethan Drama*, by Olive Mary Busby]

'Ulysses, Order, and Myth', *Dial*, lxxv/5 (Nov 1923), 480 [A review of
Ulysses, by James Joyce; Reprinted in *Dial*, i/1 (Fall, 1959), 153]

'Lettre d'Angleterre', *Nouvelle Revue Française*, xxi/122 (1 Nov 1923),
619

'Marianne Moore', *Dial*, lxxv/6 (Dec 1923), 594 [A review of *Poems*
and *Marriage*, by Marianne Moore]

'Four Elizabethan Dramatists: A Preface', *Criterion*, ii/6 (Feb 1924),
115 [Reprinted in *Selected Essays, 1917–1932*, 1932]

'A Commentary', *Criterion*, ii/7 (April 1924), 231 [Signed 'Crites']

'A Commentary', *Criterion*, ii/8 (July 1924), 371 [Signed 'Crites']

[A review of] *The Growth of Civilization* and *The Origin of Magic and
Religion* [By W. J. Perry], *Criterion*, ii/8 (July 1924), 489

'A Commentary', *Criterion*, iii/9 (Oct 1924), 1 [Signed 'Crites']

'Poème', *Commerce*, iii (Winter 1924/1925), 9 [Reprinted as Part I of
'The Hollow Men']

'Doris's Dream Songs, I–III', *Chapbook*, 39 (Nov 1924), 36 [Eyes that
last I saw in tears; The wind sprang up at four o'clock; This is the
dead land; The first two poems reprinted in *Poems 1909–1935* and
in other collections as 'Minor Poems'; The third poem reprinted as
Part III of 'The Hollow Men']

'A Commentary', *Criterion*, iii/10 (Jan 1925), 161 [Signed 'Crites']

'Three Poems', *Criterion*, iii/10 (Jan 1925), 170 [Eyes I dare not meet
in dreams; Eyes that last I saw in tears; The eyes are not here; The
first and third poems reprinted as Parts ii and iv of 'The Hollow Men']

'On the Eve, A Dialogue', *Criterion*, iii/10 (Jan 1925), 278 [Written by
Vivienne Eliot; Extensively revised by T. S. Eliot]

'The Hollow Men, I–III', *Dial*, lxxviii/3 (March 1925), 193 [Reprinted
as Parts i–ii and iv of 'The Hollow Men']

'A Commentary', *Criterion*, iii/11 (April 1925), 341

'The Ballet', *Criterion*, iii/11 (April 1925), 441 [A review of *The Dance:
An Historical Survey of Dancing in Europe*, by Cecil J. Sharpe and
A. P. Oppé; *Mudras: The Ritual Hand Poses of the Buddha Priests
and Shiva Priests*, by Tyra de Kleen]

'Recontre', *Nouvelle Revue Française*, xii/139 (1 April 1925), 657 [A tribute to Jacques Rivière]

'English Satire', *Times Literary Supplement*, 1247 (10 Dec 1925), 854 [A review of *English Satire and Satirists*, by Hugh Walker; Unsigned]

'An Italian Critic on Donne and Crashaw', *Times Literary Supplement*, 1248 (17 Dec 1925), 878 [A review of *Secentismo e marinismo in Inghilterra: John Donne – Richard Crashaw*, by Mario Praz; Unsigned]

'Shakespeare and Montaigne', *Times Literary Supplement*, 1249 (24 Dec 1925), 895 [A review of *Shakespeare's Debt to Montaigne*, by George Coffin Taylor; Unsigned]

'Wanley and Chapman', *Times Literary Supplement*, 1250 (31 Dec 1925), 907 [A review of *Essays and Studies by Members of the English Association, Volume XI*, ed. by Oliver Elton; Unsigned]

'The Idea of a Literary Review', *Criterion*, iv/1 (Jan 1926), 1

'A Popular Shakespeare', *Times Literary Supplement*, 1255 (4 Feb 1926), 76 [A review of *The Works of Shakespeare, Chronologically Arranged*, with introduction by Charles Whibley; Unsigned]

'A Commentary', *Criterion*, iv/2 (April 1926), 221 [Unsigned]

'Mr. Robertson and Mr. Shaw', *Criterion*, iv/2 (April 1926), 389 [A review of *Mr. Shaw.and 'The Maid'*, by the Rt. Hon. J. M. Robertson]

[A review of] *All God's Chillun Got Wings, Desire under the Elms, and Welded* [By Eugene O'Neill], *Criterion*, iv/2 (April 1926), 395

'A Commentary', *Criterion*, iv/3 (June 1926), 417 [Unsigned]

'English Verse Satire', *Times Literary Supplement*, 1273 (24 June 1926), 429 [A review of *A Book of English Verse Satire*, ed. by A. G. Barnes; Unsigned]

'The Author of "The Burning Babe"', *Times Literary Supplement*, 1278 (29 July 1926), 508 [A review of *The Book of Robert Southwell*, by Christobel M. Hood; Unsigned]

'Plague Pamphlets', *Times Literary Supplement*, 1279 (5 Aug 1926), 522 [A review of *The Plague Pamphlets of Thomas Dekker*, ed. by F. P. Wilson; Unsigned]

'Creative Criticism', *Times Literary Supplement*, 1280 (12 Aug 1926), 535 [A review of *Creative Criticism: Essays on the Unity of Genius and Taste*, by J. E. Spingarn; Unsigned]

'Chaucer's "Troilus"', *Times Literary Supplement*, 1281 (19 Aug 1926), 547 [A review of *The Book of Troilus and Criseyde by Geoffrey Chaucer*, ed. by Robert K. Root; Unsigned]

'American Prose', *Times Literary Supplement*, 1283 (2 Sept 1926), 577 [A review of *The Outlook for American Prose*, by Joseph W. Beach; *S. P. E. Tract No XXIV: Notes on Relative Clauses*, by Otto Jespersen; *American Slang*, by Fred N. Scott; Unsigned]

'Lancelot Andrewes', *Times Literary Supplement*, 1286 (23 Sept 1926), 621 [Unsigned; Reprinted in *For Lancelot Andrewes*, 1928]

'A Commentary', *Criterion*, iv/4 (Oct 1926), 627 [Unsigned]

'Fragment of a Prologue', *Criterion*, iv/4 (Oct 1926), 713 [Reprinted as the first section of *Sweeney Agonistes*, 1932]

'Mr. Read and M. Fernandez', *Criterion*, iv/4 (Oct 1926), 751 [A review of *Reason and Romanticism*, by Herbert Read; *Messages*, by Ramon Fernandez]

'Hooker, Hobbes, and Others', *Times Literary Supplement*, 1932 (11 Nov 1926), 789 [A review of *The Social and Political Ideas of Some Great Thinkers of the Sixteenth and Seventeenth Centuries: A Series of Lectures*, ed. by F. J. C. Hearnshaw; Unsigned]

'Massinger', *Times Literary Supplement*, 1294 (18 Nov 1926), 814 [A review of *Etude sur la collaboration de Massinger avec Fletcher et son groupe*, by Maurice Chelli; *Massinger's A New Way to Pay Old Debts*, by A. W. Reed; Unsigned]

'Sir John Davies', *Times Literary Supplement*, 1297 (9 Dec 1926), 906 [Unsigned] [Reprinted in *On Poetry and Poets*, 1957]

'Medieval Philosophy', *Times Literary Supplement*, 1298 (16 Dec 1926), 929 [A review of *History of Mediaeval Philosophy*, by Maurice de Wulf; Unsigned]

'Whitman and Tennyson', *Nation & Athenaeum*, xl/11 (18 Dec 1926), 426 [A review of *Whitman: An Interpretation in Narrative*, by Emory Holloway]

'A Commentary', *Criterion*, v/1 (Jan 1927), 1 [Unsigned]

'Poetry and Religion by Jacques Maritain, I', *Criterion*, v/1 (Jan 1927), 7 [Translated by T. S. Eliot]

'Fragment of an Agon', *Criterion*, v/1 (Jan 1927), 74 [Reprinted as the second section of *Sweeney Agonistes*, 1932]

'Grammar and Usage', *Criterion*, v/1 (Jan 1927), 121 [A review of *Modern English Usage*, by H. W. Fowler; *The Philosophy of Grammar*, by Otto Jespersen; *A Grammar of Late Modern English*, by H. Poutsma; *Le langage*, by J. Vendryes]

'Homage to Wilkie Collins', *Criterion*, v/1 (Jan 1927), 139 [A review of nine mystery novels]

'A Note on Poetry and Belief', *Enemy*, 1 (Jan 1927), 15

'The Phoenix Nest', *Times Literary Supplement*, 1303 (20 Jan 1927), 41 [A review of *The Phoenix Nest, Reprinted from the Original Edition of 1593*; Unsigned]

'Charleston, Hey! Hey!', *Nation & Athenaeum*, xl/17 (29 Jan 1927), 595 [A review of *The Future of Futurism*, by John Rodker; *Composition as Explanation*, by Gertrude Stein; *Pomona: or The Futura of English*, by Basil de Selincourt; *Catchwords and Claptrap*, by Rose Macaulay]

'The Problems of the Shakespeare Sonnets', *Nation & Athenaeum*, xl/19 (12 Feb 1927), 664 [A review of *The Problems of the Shakespeare Sonnets*, by J. M. Robertson]

'Literature, Science, and Dogma', *Dial*, lxxxii/3 (March 1927), 239 [A review of *Science and Poetry*, by I. A. Richards]

'A Study of Marlowe', *Times Literary Supplement*, 1309 (3 March 1927), 140 [A review of *Christopher Marlowe*, by U. M. Ellis-Fermor; Unsigned]

'Spinoza', *Times Literary Supplement*, 1316 (21 April 1927), 275 [A

review of *The Oldest Biography of Spinoza*, ed. by A. Wolf; Unsigned]
'A Commentary', *Criterion*, v/2 (May 1927), 187 [Unsigned]
'Poetry and Religion by Jacques Maritain, II', *Criterion*, v/2 (May 1927), 214 [Translated by T. S. Eliot]
'Popular Theologians: Mr. Wells, Mr. Belloc and Mr. Murray', *Criterion*, v/2 (May 1927), 253 [A review of *The Life of Jesus*, by J. Middleton Murry; *A Companion to Mr. Wells's Outline of History*, by Hilaire Belloc; *Mr. Belloc Objects*, by H. G. Wells; *Mr. Belloc Still Objects*, by Hilaire Belloc; *The Anglo-Catholic Faith*, by T. A. Lacey; *Modernism in the English Church*, by Percy Gardner
'Poet and Saint . . . ', *Dial*, lxxxii/5 (May 1927), 424 [A review of *Baudelaire: Prose and Poetry*, translated by Arthur Symons; Reprinted as 'Baudelaire in Our Time' in *For Lancelot Andrewes*, 1928]
'Le roman anglais contemporain', *Nouvelle Revue Française*, xxviii/164 (1 May 1927), 669
'Israfel', *Nation & Athenaeum*, xli/7 (21 May 1927), 219 [A review of *Israfel: The Life and Times of Edgar Allan Poe*, by Hervey Allen; *Poems and Miscellanies of Edgar Allan Poe*, ed. by R. Brimley Johnson; *Tales of Mystery*, by Edgar Allan Poe]
'A Commentary', *Criterion*, v/3 (June 1927), 283 [Unsigned]
'Recent Detective Fiction', *Criterion*, v/3 (June 1927), 359 [A review of 16 detective novels; *Problems of Modern American Crime*, by Veronica and Paul King
'Nicolo Machiavelli', *Times Literary Supplement*, 1324 (16 June 1927), 413 [Unsigned; Reprinted in *For Lancelot Andrewes*, 1928]
'Thomas Middleton', *Times Literary Supplement*, 1326 (30 June 1927), 445 [Unsigned; Reprinted in *For Lancelot Andrewes*, 1928]
'A Commentary', *Criterion*, vi/1 (July 1927), 1 [Unsigned]
'Political Theorists', *Criterion*, vi/1 (July 1927), 69 [A review of *A Defence of Conservatism*, by Anthony M. Ludovici; *The Outline of Sanity*, by G. K. Chesteron; *The Servile State*, by Hillaire Belloc; *The Conditions of Industrial Peace*, by J. A. Hobson]
'Archbishop Bramhall', *Theology*, xv/85 (July, 1927), 11 [A review of Archbishop Bramhall, by W. J. Sparrow-Simpson; Reprinted as 'John Bramhall' in *For Lancelot Andrewes*, 1928]
'Plays of Ben Jonson', *Times Literary Supplement*, 1329 (21 July 1927), 500 [A review of *Ben Jonson*, ed. by C. H. Herford and Percy Simpson; *Eastward Hoe*, ed. by Julia H. Harris; *The Alchemist*, replica of the first quarto; Unsigned]
'A Commentary', *Criterion*, vi/2 (Aug 1927), 97 [Unsigned]
'Why Mr. Russell Is a Christian', *Criterion*, vi/2 (Aug 1927), 177 [A review of *Why I Am Not a Christian*, by the Hon. Bertrand Russell]
'Wilkie Collins and Dickens', *Times Literary Supplement*, 1331 (4 Aug 1927), 525 (Unsigned] [Reprinted in *Selected Essays, 1919–1932*, 1932]
'The Twelfth Century', *Times Literary Supplement*, 1332 (11 Aug 1927), 542 [A review of *The Renaissance of the Twelfth Century*, by Charles Homer Haskins; Unsigned]

[A review of] *The Playgoers' Handbook to the English Renaissance Drama* [By Agnes Mure Mackenize], *Times Literary Supplement*, 1334 (25 Aug 1927), 577 [Unsigned]

'Commentary', *Criterion*, vi/3 (Sept 1927), 193 [Unsigned]

'Concerning "Intuition" by Charles Mauron', *Criterion*, vi/3 (Sept 1927), 229 [Translated by T. S. Eliot]

'The Silurist', *Dial*, lxxxiii/3 (Sept 1927), 259 [A review of *On the Poems of Henry Vaughan: Characteristics and Intimations*, by Edmund Blunden]

'The Mysticism of Blake', *Nation & Athenaeum*, xli/24 (17 Sept 1927), 779 [A review of six books by or about William Blake]

'A Commentary', *Criterion*, vi/4 (Oct 1927), 289 [Unsigned]

'A Note on Intelligence and Intuition by Ramon Fernandez', *Criterion*, vi/4 (Oct 1927), 332 [Translated by T. S. Eliot]

'Mr. Middleton Murry's Synthesis', *Criterion*, vi/4 (Oct 1927), 340

'Parnassus Biceps', *Times Literary Supplement*, 1342 (20 Oct 1927), 734 [A review of *Parnassus Biceps; or Several Choice Pieces of Poetry*, ed. by G. Thorn-Drury; unsigned]

'A Scholar's Essays', *Times Literary Supplement*, 1343 (27 Oct 1927), 757 [A review of *Nine Essays*, by Arthur Platt; Unsigned]

'A Commentary', *Criterion*, vi/5 (Nov 1927), 385 [Unsigned]

'A Commentary', *Criterion*, vi/6 (Dec 1927), 481 [Unsigned]

'Stage Studies', *Times Literary Supplement*, 1349 (8 Dec 1927), 927 [A review of *Pre-Restoration Stage Studies* and *The Physical Conditions of the Elizabethan Public Playhouse*, by William J. Lawrence; Unsigned]

'Salutation', *Saturday Review of Literature*, iv/20 (10 Dec 1927), 429 [Reprinted as Part II of *Ash-Wednesday*, 1930]

'Bradley's "Ethical Studies"', *Times Literary Supplement*, 1352 (29 Dec 1927), 981 [Unsigned; Reprinted as 'Francis Herbert Bradley' in *For Lancelot Andrewes*, 1928]

'Mr. Chesterton and Stevenson', *Nation & Athenaeum*, xlii/3 (31 Dec 1927), 516 [A review of *Robert Louis Stevenson*, by G. K. Chesterton]

'A Commentary', *Criterion*, vii/1 (Jan 1928), 1 [Unsigned]

'Prologue to an Essay on Criticism by Charles Maurras, I', *Criterion*, vii/1 (Jan 1928), 5 [Translated by T. S. Eliot]

'Isolated Superiority', *Dial*, lxxxiv/1 (Jan 1928), 4 [A review of *Personae: The Collected Poems of Ezra Pound*]

'A Commentary', *Criterion*, vii/2 (Feb 1928), 97 [Unsigned]

'From "Anabase" by St. J. Perse', *Criterion*, vii/2 (Feb 1928), 137 [Translated by T. S. Eliot]

'An Emotional Unity', *Dial*, lxxxiv/2 (Feb 1928), 109 [A review of *Selected Letters of Baron Friedrich von Hügel (1896–1924)*, ed. by Bernard Holland]

'Perch' io non spero', *Commerce*, xv (Spring 1928), 5 [Reprinted in English as Part I of *Ash-Wednesday*, 1930]

'A Commentary', *Criterion*, vii/3 (March 1928), 193 [Unsigned]

'The *Action Francaise*, M. Maurras and Mr. Ward', *Criterion*, vii/3 (March 1928), 195

'Prologue to an Essay on Criticism by Charles Maurras, II' *Criterion*, vii/3 (March 1928), 204 [Translated by T. S. Eliot]

'The Poems English Latin and Greek of Richard Crashaw', *Dial*, lxxxiv/3 (March 1928), 246 [A review of *The Poems English Latin and Greek of Richard Crashaw*, ed. by L. C. Martin; Reprinted as 'A Note on Richard Crashaw' in *For Lancelot Andrewes*, 1928]

'A Commentary', *Criterion*, vii/4 (June 1928), 1 [Unsigned]

'L'Action Francaise . . . A Reply to Mr. Ward', *Criterion*, vii/4 (June 1928), 84

'Mr Lucas's Webster', *Criterion*, vii/4 (June 1928), 155 [A review of *The Complete Works of John Webster*, ed. by F. L. Lucas]

'The Oxford Jonson', *Dial*, lxxxv/1 (July 1928), 65 [A review of *Ben Jonson*, ed. by C. H. Herford and Percy Simpson]

'The Humanism of Irving Babbitt', *Forum*, lxxx/1 (July 1928), 37 [Reprinted in *For Lancelot Andrewes*, 1928]

'Sir John Denham', *Times Literary Supplement*, 1379 (5 July 1928), 501 [A review of *The Poetical Works of Sir John Denham*, ed. by Theodore H. Banks; Unsigned]

'An Extempore Exhumation', *Nation & Athenaeum*, xliii/14 (7 July 1928), 470 [A review of *The Skull of Swift*, by Shane Leslie]

'A Commentary', *Criterion*, viii/30 (Sept 1928), 1 [Unsigned]

'Civilisation: 1928 Model', *Criterion*, viii/30 (Sept 1928), 161 [A review of *Civilization*, by Clive Bell]

'The Golden Ass of Apuleius', *Dial*, lxxxv/3 (Sept 1928), 254 [A review of *The Golden Ass of Apuleius, the Adlington Translation*]

'Three Reformers', *Times Literary Supplement*, 1397 (8 Nov 1928), 818 [A review of *Three Reformers: Luther, Descartes, Rousseau*, by Jacques Maritain; Unsigned]

'A Commentary', *Criterion*, viii/31 (Dec 1928), 185 [Unsigned]

'Fustel de Coulanges by Pierre Gaxotte', *Criterion*, viii/31 (Dec 1928), 258 [Translated by T. S. Eliot]

'The Literature of Fascism', *Criterion*, viii/31 (Dec 1928), 280

'Freud's Illusions', *Criterion*, viii/31 (Dec 1928), 350 [A review of *The Future of an Illusion*, by Sigmund Freud]

'Elizabeth and Essex', *Times Literary Supplement*, 1401 (6 Dec 1928), 959 [A review of *Elizabeth and Essex: A Tragic History*, by Lytton Strachey; Unsigned]

'American Critics', *Times Literary Supplement*, 1406 (10 Jan 1929), 24 [A review of *The Reinterpretation of American Literature*, ed. by Norman Foerster; Unsigned]

'Introduction to Goethe', *Nation & Athenaeum*, xliv/15 (12 Jan 1929), 527 [A review of *Goethe and Faust: An Interpretation*, by F. Melian Stawell and G. Lowes Dickinson; *Goethe's Faust*, translated by Anna Swanwick]

'Turbeville's Ovid', *Times Literary Supplement*, 1407 (17 Jan 1929), 40 [A review of *The Heroycall Epistles of Ovid, Translated into*

English Verse by George Turbeville, ed. by Frederick Boas', Unsigned]

'Mr. P. E. More's Essays', *Times Literary Supplement*, 1412 (21 Feb 1929), 136 [A review of *The Demon of the Absolute*, by Paul Elmer More; Unsigned]

'The Latin Tradition', *Times Literary Supplement*, 1415 (14 March 1929), 200 [A review of *Founders of the Middle Ages*, by Edward Kennard Rand; Unsigned]

'A Commentary', *Criterion*, viii/32 (April 1929), 377 [Unsigned]

'Sherlock Holmes and His Times', *Criterion*, viii/32 (April 1929), 552 [review of *The Complete Sherlock Holmes Short Stories*, by Sir Arthur Conan Doyle; *The Leavenworth Case*, by Anna K. Green]

Letter, *Little Review*, xii/2 (May 1929), 90 [On the discontinuance of the periodical]

'The Tudor Translators', *Listener*, i/22 (12 June 1929), 833

'The Elizabethan Grub Street', *Listener*, i/23 (19 June 1929), 853

'A Commentary', *Criterion*, viii/33 (July 1929), 575 [Unsigned]

'Mr. Barnes and Mr. Rowse', *Criterion*, viii/33 (July 1929), 682

'The Prose of the Preacher: The Sermons of Donne', *Listener*, ii/25 (3 July 1929), 22

'Elizabethan Travellers' Tales', *Listener*, ii/26 (10 July 1929), 59

'The Tudor Biographers', *Listener*, ii/27 (17 July 1929), 94

'Som de l'Escalina', *Commerce*, xxi (Autumn 1929), 99 [Reprinted in English as Part iii of *Ash-Wednesday*, 1930]

'A Commentary', *Criterion*, ix/34 (Oct 1929), 1 [Unsigned]

'A Commentary', *Criterion*, ix/35 (Jan 1930), 181 [Unsigned]

'A Humanist Theory of Value by Ramon Fernandez', *Criterion*, ix/35 (Jan 1930), 228 [Translated by T. S. Eliot]

[A review of *Baudelaire and the Symbolists: Five Essays* by Peter Quennell, *Criterion*, ix/35 (Jan 1930), 357

'Thinking in Verse: A Survey of Early Seventeenth-Century Poetry', *Listener*, iii/61 (12 March 1930), 441

'Rhyme and Reason: The Poetry of John Donne', *Listener*, iii/62 (19 March 1930), 502

'The Devotional Poets of the Seventeenth Century: Donne, Herbert, Crashaw', *Listener*, iii/63 (26 March 1930), 552

'A Commentary', *Criterion*, ix/36 (April 1930), 381 [Unsigned]

'Mystic and Politician as Poet: Vaughan, Traherne, Marvell, Milton', *Listener*, iii/64 (2 April 1930), 590

'The Minor Metaphysicals: From Cowley to Dryden', *Listener*, iii/65 (9 April 1930), 641

'John Dryden', *Listener*, iii/66 (16 April 1930), 688

'A Commentary', *Criterion*, ix/37 (July 1930), 587 [Unsigned]

'On Reading Einstein by Charles Mauron', *Criterion*, x/38 (Oct 1930), 23 [Translated by T. S. Eliot]

'From a Distinguished Former St. Louisan', *St. Louis Post—Dispatch*, (5 Oct 1930) [A letter from T. S. Eliot concerning his memories of St. Louis]

'Cyril Tourneur', *Times Literary Supplement*, 1502 (13 Nov 1930), 925

[A review of *The Works of Cyril Tourneur*, ed. by Allardyce Nicoll; unsigned; Reprinted in *Selected Essays, 1919–1932*, [1932]
'A Commentary', *Criterion*, x/39 (Jan 1931), 307
'A Commentary', *Criterion*, x/40 (April 1931), 481
'John Dryden, I: The Poet Who Gave The English Speech', *Listener*, v/118 (15 April 1931), 621[Reprinted in *John Dryden: The Poet, the Dramatist, the Critic*, 1932]
'John Dryden, II: Dryden the Dramatist', *Listener*, v/119 (22 April 1931), 681 [Reprinted in *John Dryden: The Poet, the Dramatist, the Critic*, 1932]
'John Dryden, III: Dryden the Critic, Defender of Sanity', Listener, v/120 (29 April 1931), 724 [Reprinted in *John Dryden: The Poet, the Dramatist, the Critic*, 1932]
'A Commentary', *Criterion*, x/41 (July 1931) 709
[A review of] *Son of Woman: The Story of D. H. Lawrence* [By John Middleton Murry], *Criterion*, x/41 (July 1931), 768
'Thomas Heywood', *Times Literary Supplement*, 1539 (30 July 1931), 589 [A review of *Thomas Heywood: Playwright and Miscellanist*, by Arthur M. Clark; Unsigned; Reprinted in *Selected Essays, 1917–1932*, 1932]
'A Commentary', *Criterion*, xi/42 (Oct 1931), 65
'A Commentary', *Criterion*, xi/43 (Jan 1932), 268
'Christianity and Communism', *Listener*, vii/166 (16 March 1932), 382
'Religion and Science: A Phantom Dilemma', *Listener*, vii/167 (23 March 1932), 428
'The Search for Moral Sanction', *Listener*, vii/168 (30 March 1932), 445
'A Commentary', *Criterion*, xi/44 (April 1932), 467
'Building up the Christian World', *Listener*, vii/169 (6 April 1932), 501
'John Ford', *Times Literary Supplement*, 1579 (5 May 1932), 317 [A review of *Materials for the Study of the Old English Drama, New Series, First Volume: John Ford's Dramatic Works, Volume II*, ed. by H. de Vocht; Unsigned; Reprinted in *Selected Essays, 1917–1932*, 1932]
'A Commentary', *Criterion*, xi/45 (July 1932), 676
'A Commentary', *Criterion*, xii/46 (Oct 1932), 73
'Five-Finger Exercises', *Criterion*, xii/47 (Jan 1933), 220 [Lines to a Persian Cat; Lines to a Yorkshire Terrier; Lines to a Duck in the Park; Lines for Ralph Hodgson Esqre.; Lines for Cuscuscaraway and Mirza Murad Ali Beg]
'A Commentary', *Criterion*, xii/47 (Jan 1933), 244
'A Commentary', *Criterion*, xii/48 (April 1933), 468
'A Commentary', *Criterion*, xii/49 (July 1933), 642
'A Commentary', *Criterion*, xiii/50 (Oct 1933), 115 [Reprinted in *Irving Babbitt, Man and Teacher*, 1941]
[A review of] *The Name and Nature of Poetry* [by A. E. Housman], *Criterion*, xiii/50 (Oct 1933), 151
'The Modern Dilemma', *Christian Register*, cll/41 (19 Oct 1933), 675 [An address to a meeting of Unitarian clergymen in Boston]

Works List

'A Commentary', *Criterion*, xiii/51 (Jan 1934), 270

'Mr. Eliot's Virginian Lectures', *New English Weekly*, iv/22 (15 March 1934), 528 [A reply to a review by Ezra Pound of *After Strange Gods*]

'A Commentary', *Criterion*, xiii/52 (April 1934), 451

'Words for Music: New Hampshire; Virginia', *Virginia Quarterly Review*, x/2 (April 1934), 200 [Reprinted as 'Landscapes, I–II']

'Mr. T. S. Eliot's Quandaries', *New English Weekly*, iv/26 (12 April 1934), 622 [A further reply to Ezra Pound]

'Modern Heresies', *New English Weekly*, v/3 (3 May 1934), 71

'The Use of Poetry', *New English Weekly*, v/9 (14 June 1934), 215 [A further reply to Ezra Pound; Signed 'Possum']

'A Commentary', *Criterion*, xiii/53 (July 1934), 624

[A review of] *The Oxford Handbook of Religious Knowledge*, *Criterion*, xiii/53 (July 1934), 709 [Signed, erroneously, 'Thomas McGreevy']

[A review of] *The Mystical Doctrine of St. John of the Cross*, *Criterion*, xiii/53 (July 1934), 709 [Signed, erroneously, 'Thomas McGreevy']

'John Marston', *Times Literary Supplement*, 1695 (26 July 1934), 517 [A review of *The Plays of John Marston*, ed. by H. Harvey Wood; *The Malcontent*, ed. by G. B. Harrison; Unsigned; Reprinted in *Elizabethan Essays*, 1934]

'A Commentary', *Criterion*, xiv/54 (Oct 1934), 86

'Orage: Memories', *New English Weekly*, vi/5 (15 Nov 1934), 100 [A tribute to A. R. Orage]

'A Commentary', *Criterion*, xiv/55 (Jan 1935), 260

'Notes on the Way', *Time and Tide*, xvi/1 (5 Jan 1935), 6

'Dowson's Poems', *Times Literary Supplement*, 1719 (10 Jan 1935), 21

'Notes on the Way', *Time and Tide*, xvi/2 (12 Jan 1935), 33

'Notes on the Way', *Time and Tide*, xvi/3 (19 Jan 1935), 88

'Notes on the Way', *Time and Tide*, xvi/4 (26 Jan 1935) 118

'A Commentary', *Criterion*, xiv/56 (April 1935), 431

'Views and Reviews', *New English Weekly*, vii/8 (6 June 1935), 151 [On *A Short Introduction to the History of Human Stupidity*, by Walter P. Pitkin]

'Views and Reviews', *New English Weekly*, vii/10 (20 June 1935), 190 [On prose writers]

'A Commentary', *Criterion*, xiv/57 (July 1935), 610 [On W. B. Yeats; Rev. and reprinted as 'W. B. Yeats at 70']

'Views and Reviews', *New English Weekly*, vii/18 (12 Sept 1935), 351

'A Commentary', *Criterion*, xv/58 (Oct 1935), 65

'Rannoch, by Glencoe', *New English Weekly*, viii/1 (17 Oct 1935), 10 [Reprinted as 'Landscapes, IV']

'Views and Reviews', *New English Weekly*, viii/4 (7 Nov 1935), 71 [On *Selected Essays and Critical Writings*, by A. R. Orage]

'Words for an Old Man', *New English Weekly*, viii/7 (28 Nov 1935), 131 [Reprinted as 'Lines for an Old Man']

'Stilton Cheese', *Times* (29 Nov 1935), 15

'Cape Ann', *New Democracy*, v/8 (15 Dec 1935), 137 [Reprinted as 'Landscapes, V']

'A Commentary', *Criterion*, xv/59 (Jan 1936), 265

[A review of] *Totem: The Exploitation of Youth* [By Harold Stovin], *Criterion*, xv/59 (Jan 1936), 363 [unsigned]

[A review of] *Selected Shelburne Essays* [By Paul Elmer More], *Criterion*, xv/59 (Jan 1936), 363 [Unsigned]

'A Commentary', *Criterion*, xv/60 (April 1936), 458

'A Commentary', *Criterion*, xv/61 (July 1936), 663

'Mr. Murry's Shakespeare', *Criterion*, xv/61 (July 1936), 708 [A review of *Shakespeare*, by John Middleton Murry]

'A Commentary', *Criterion*, xvi/62 (Oct 1936), 63

'The Need for Poetic Drama', *Listener*, xvi/411 (25 Nov 1936), 994 [A Schools Broadcast to Sixth Forms]

'A Commentary', *Criterion*, xvi/63 (Jan 1937), 289

'The Church's Message to the World', *Listener*, xvii/423 (17 Feb 1937), 373 [Reprinted as an appendix to *The Idea of a Christian Society*, 1939]

'A Commentary', *Criterion*, xvi/64 (April 1937), 469

'Nightwood', *Criterion*, xvi/64 (April 1937), 560 [A review of *Nightwood*, by Djuna Barnes; A reprint of T. S. Eliot's introduction to the first American edition of the book]

'A Commentary', *Criterion*, xvi/65 (July 1937), 666

'The Church and the World: Problem of Common Social Action', *Times*, (17 July 1937), 18 [An address delivered at Oxford, 16 June]

'Religious Drama: Mediaeval and Modern', *University of Edinburgh Journal*, ix/1 (Autumn 1937), 8 [An address delivered to the Friends of Rochester Cathedral; Pubd 1954]

'A Commentary', *Criterion*, xvii/66 (Oct 1937), 81

'An Anglican Platonist: The Conversion of Elmer More', *Times Literary Supplement*, 1865 (30 Oct 1937), 792 [A review of *Pages from an Oxford Diary*, by Paul Elmer More; Unsigned]

'A Commentary', *Criterion*, xvii/67 (Jan 1938), 254

'A Commentary', *Criterion*, xvii/68 (April 1938), 478

'A Commentary', *Criterion*, xvii/69 (July 1938), 686

'Five Points on Dramatic Writing', *Townsman*, i/3 (July 1938), 10

'Professor H. H. Joachim', *Times* (4 Aug 1938), 12 [An obituary letter]

'A Commentary', *Criterion*, xviii/70 (Oct 1938), 58

'Eight Poems', *Harvard Advocate*, cxxv/3 (Dec 1938), 9 [When We Came Home across the Hill; Before Morning; Circe's Palace; The Moonflower opens to the Moth; Nocturne; Humoresque; Spleen; Reprinted in the same periodical, Nov 1948]

'A Commentary: Last Words', *Criterion*, xviii/71 (Jan 1939), 269 [Reprinted as 'A Valedictorian' in *Selected Prose*, 1953]

'A Liberal Manifesto', *Church Times*, cxxi/3966 (27 Jan 1939), 78

'A Commentary: That Poetry Is Made with Words', *New English Weekly*, xv/2 (27 April 1939), 27 [On *Situation de la poésie*, by Jacques and Raissa Maritain]

'A Commentary: On Reading Official Reports', *New English Weekly*, xv/4 (11 May 1939), 61 [On the *Report of the Consultative Committee on Secondary Education*, pubd by the Board of Education]

'Symposium: The Idea of a Christian Society', *Purpose*, xi/3 (July/Sept 1939), 162 [Reprinted as Chapter 1 of *The Idea of a Christian Society*, 1939]

'A Commentary', *New English Weekly*, xv/25 (5 Oct 1939), 331 [On *The Religious Prospect*, by V. A. Demant]

'A Sub-Pagan Society?', *New English Weekly*, xvi/9 (14 Dec 1939), 125 [On a review by Maurice B. Reckitt of *The Idea of a Christian Society*]

'Views and Reviews: Journalists of Yesterday and Today', *New English Weekly*, xvi/16 (8 Feb 1940), 237

'Views and Reviews: On Going West', *New English Weekly*, xvi/17 (15 Feb 1940), 251

'East Coker', *New English Weekly*, xvi/22 (21 March 1940), 325 [Reprinted separately in 1940 and in later collections as the second of the 'Four Quartets']

'The Poetry of W. B. Yeats', *Purpose*, xii/3–4 (July/Dec 1940), 115 [The first Annual Yeats Lecture, delivered to the Friends of the Irish Academy at the Abbey Theatre, June 1940; Reprinted as 'Yeats' in *Selected Prose*, 1953]

Christian News–Letter, 42 (14 Aug 1940) [The entire issue written by T. S. Eliot, as guest-editor]

Christian News–Letter, 43 (21 Aug 1940) [The entire issue written by T. S. Eliot, as guest-editor]

Christian News–Letter, 44 (28 Aug 1940) [The entire issue written by T. S. Eliot, as guest-editor]

'A Commentary', *New English Weekly*, xviii/7 (5 Dec 1940), 75 [On Ronald Duncan's periodical, *Townsman*]

'Views and Reviews: Waiting at the Church', *New English Weekly*, xviii/9 (19 Dec 1940), 99

'The Dry Salvages', *New English Weekly*, xviii/19 (27 Feb 1941), 217 [Reprinted separately in 1941 and in later collections as the third of the 'Four Quartets']

'A Message to the Fish', *Horizon*, iii/15 (March 1941), 73 [On the obituary notice of James Joyce in the *Times*, 14 Jan 1941]

'Towards a Christian Britain', *Listener*, xxv/639 (10 April 1941), 524

'Virginia Woolf', *Horizon*, iii/17 (May 1941), 313

'Views and Reviews: Basic Revelation', *New English Weekly*, xix/10 (26 June 1941), 101 [On the New Testament in Basic English]

Christian News–Letter, 97 (3 Sept 1941) [The entire issue written by T. S. Eliot, as guest-editor]

'Russian Ballet', *Times*, (10 Dec 1941), 5

Christian News–Letter, 141 (8 July 1942) [The entire issue written by T. S. Eliot, as guest-editor]

'T. S. Eliot on Poetry in Wartime', *Common Sense*, xi/10 (Oct 1942), 351 [A radio address to Swedish audiences]

'Little Gidding', *New English Weekly*, xxi/26 (15 Oct 1942), 213 [Reprinted separately in 1942 and in later collections as the last of the 'Four Quartets']

'Notes towards a Definition of Culture, I', *New English Weekly*, xxii/14 (21 Jan 1943), 117
'Notes towards a Definition of Culture, II', *New English Weekly*, xxii/15 (28 Jan 1943), 129
'Notes towards a Definition of Culture, III', *New English Weekly*, xxii/16 (4 Feb 1943), 136
'Notes towards a Definition of Culture, IV', *New English Weekly*, xxii/17 (11 Feb 1943), 145 [All four parts rev. and pubd in *Prospect for Christendom*, 1945 and in *Notes towards the Definition of Culture*, 1948]
'The Approach to James Joyce', *Listener*, xxx/770 (14 Oct 1943), 446
'The Social Function of Poetry', *Norseman*, i/6 (Nov 1943), 449 [An extract from a lecture given at the British—Norwegian Institute]
'Responsibility and Power', *Christian News—Letter*, 196 (1 Dec 1943), supplement
'Aristocracy', *Times*, (17 April 1944), 5
'Books for the Freed World', *Times*, (8 May 1944), 5
'What France Means to You', *La France Libre*, viii/44 (15 June 1944), 94 [T. S. Eliot's contribution to a series, ed. by Raymond Mortimer]
'The Responsibility of the Man of Letters in the Cultural Restoration of Europe', *Norseman*, ii/4 (July/Aug 1944), 243 [Reprinted as 'The Man of Letters and the Future of Europe' in *Horizon*, Dec 1944]
'What Is Minor Poetry?', *Welsh Review*, 4 (Dec 1944), 256 [Address delivered before the Association of Bookmen of Swansea and West Wales, 26 Sept 1944; Reprinted in *On Poetry and Poets*, 1957]
'Four Quartets', *New English Weekly*, xxvi/15 (25 Jan 1945), 112 [A letter concerning 'Four Quartets']
'The Germanization of England', *New English Weekly*, xxvi/21 (8 March 1945), 167
'Full Employment and the Responsibility of Christians', *Christian News-Letter*, 230 (21 March 1945), 7 [Signed with the pseudonym, 'Metoikos']
'The Germanization of England', *New English Weekly*, xxvi/24 (29 March 1945), 192
'Cultural Diversity and European Unity', *Review—45*, ii/2 (Summer 1945), 61 [An address given at the Czechoslovak Institute, April 1945]
'The Social Function of Poetry', *Adelphi*, xxi/4 (July/Sept 1945), 152 [An address delivered in Paris, May 1945; modification of essay pubd in *Norseman*, Nov 1943; Reprinted in *On Poetry and Poet*, 1957)
'The Class and the Élite', *New English Review*, xi/6 (Oct 1945), 499 [Rev. and pubd as Chapter 2 of *Notes towards the Definition of Culture*, 1948]
'Mass Deportations', *Times*, (30 Oct 1945), 5
'Reflections on the Unity of European Culture, I', *Adam*, xiv/158 (May 1946), 1

'Reflections on the Unity of European Culture, II', *Adam*, xiv/159—160 (June/July 1946), 1

'Reflections on the Unity of European Culture, III', *Adam*, xiv/161 (Aug 1946), 20 [Rev. and reprinted as 'The Criterion' in the same periodical, 1953]

'Ezra Pound', *Poetry*, lxviii/6 (Sept 1946), 326—38 [Reprinted in *New English Weekly*, 31 Oct—7 Nov 1946]

'Individualists in Verse', *New English Weekly*, xxx/5 (14 Nov 1946), 52

'The Significance of Charles Williams', *Listener*, xxxvi/936 (19 Dec 1946), 894 [Rev. and reprinted as an introduction to *All Hallows Eve* by Charles Williams, 1948]

'Grant Amnesty to All War and Political Prisoners', *Catholic Herald*, (20 Dec 1946), 1 [T. S. Eliot's contribution to a symposium]

'Professor Karl Mannheim', *Times*, (25 Jan 1947), 7 [A obituary letter]

'Culture and Politics', *Adelphi*, xxiii/3 (April/June 1947), 119 [A radio talk to German audiences, March 1946; Reprinted from *Die Einheit der Europäischen Kultur*, 1946]

'UNESCO and the Philospher', *Times*, (20 Sept 1947), 5

'UNESCO and its Aims: The Definition of Culture', *Times*, (17 Oct 1947), 7

'Mr. Eliot on Milton', *Sunday Times*, (16 Nov 1947) 6

'Views and Reviews: "Our Culture"', *New English Weekly*, xxxii/21 (4 March 1948), 203 [A review of *Our Culture . . . The Edward Alleyn Lectures, 1944*]

'Naturalized Subjects', *Times*, (7 May 1948), 5

'Views and Reviews: Michael Roberts', *New English Weekly*, xxxiv/14 (13 Jan 1949), 164

'Leadership and Letters', *Milton Bulletin*, xii/1 (Feb 1949), 3 [The War Memorial Address delivered at Milton Academy, 3 Nov 1948]

'Note on Wyndham Lewis', *Time*, liii/22 (30 May 1949), 60 [An article on Lewis quotes a statement by T. S. Eliot]

'T. S. Eliot Answers Questions', *John O'London's Weekly*, lviii/1369 (19 Aug 1949), 497 [An interview by Ranjee Shahani, with T. S. Eliot's answers in direct quotation]

'Mr Ezra Pound', *New Alliance & Scots Review*, x/6 (Sept 1949), 98

'The Cocktail Party', *Life*, xxvii/13 (26 Sept 1949), 16 [A report in which 60 lines of the play are quoted]

'The Aims of Poetic Drama', *Adam*, xvii/200 (Nov 1949), 10 [An address delivered to various European audiences; Rev. and pubd as *Poetry and Drama*, 1951]

'The Human Mind Analyzed by T. S. Eliot', *New York Times Magazine*, (29 Jan 1950), 14 [145 lines from *The Cocktail Party*]

'Talk on Dante', *Italian News*, 2 (July 1950), 13 [A lecture delivered at the Italian Institute, 4 July 1950; Reprinted in *Adelphi*, First Quarter 1951, and in *Selected Prose*, 1953]

'Poetry by T. S. Eliot: An NBC Radio Discussion', *University of Chicago*

Round Table, 659 (12 Nov 1950), 1 [The entire issue devoted to a reading by T. S. Eliot of his poems, with commentary]

'The Aims of Education: Can "Education" Be Defined?', *Measure*, ii/1 (Dec 1950), 3 [A lecture delivered at University of Chicago, Nov 1950]

'The Television Habit', *Times*, (20 Dec 1950), 7

'Books of the Year Chosen by Eminent Contemporaries . . . From T. S. Eliot, O. M.', *Sunday Times*, (24 Dec 1950), 3

'Poetry and Drama', *Atlantic Monthly*, clxxxvii/2 (Feb 1951), 30 [The first Theodore Spencer Memorial Lecture delivered at Harvard University, 21 Nov 1950; Pubd 1951]

'The Aims of Education: The Interrelation of Aims', *Measure,* ii/2 (Spring 1951), 191 [A lecture delivered at University of Chicago, Nov 1950]

'The Aims of Education; The Conflict between Aims', *Measure*, ii/3 (Summer 1951), 285 [A lecture delivered at University of Chicago, Nov 1950]

'The Aims of Education: The Issue of Religion', *Measure*, ii/4 (Fall 1951), 362 [All four parts reprinted in *To Criticize the Critic and Other Writings*, 1965]

'Vergil and the Christian World', *Listener*, xlvi/1176 (13 Sept 1951), 411 [Reprinted as 'Virgil and Destiny' in *Selected Prose*, 1953]

'The Value and Use of Cathedrals in England Today', *Friends of Chichester Cathedral Annual Report*, (1950/51), 17 [An address delivered in Chichester Cathedral to the Friends of Chichester Cathedral, 16 June 1951; Pubd 1952]

'World Tribute to Bernard Shaw', *Time and Tide*, xxxii/50 (15 Dec 1951), 1231

'An Address to Members of the London Library', *Book Collector*, i/3 (Autumn 1952), 139 [An address delivered at the Annual General Meeting of Members, 22 July 1952; Pubd 1952]

'Cat Morgan's Apology through the Pen of T. S. Eliot', *Animals' Magazine*, vii/9 (Sept 1952), 4

'The Publishing of Poetry', *Bookseller*, 2450 (6 Dec 1952), 1568 [An address delivered to the Society of Young Publishers, Nov 1952]

'Charles Maurras', *Time and Tide*, xxxiv/3 (17 Jan 1953), 82

'The Confidential Clerk', *Saturday Review*, xxxvi/37 (12 Sept 1953), 44 [A review in which 32 lines of the play are quoted]

'T. S. Eliot Talks about Himself and the Drive to Create', *New York Times Book Review*, (29 Nov 1953), 5 [An interview by John Lehmann, in which T. S. Eliot's actual words are quoted]

'A Message', *London Magazine*, i/1 (Feb 1954), 1

'T. S. Eliot Turns to Comedy', *Life*, xxxvi/5 (1 Feb 1954), 62 [An article in which 47 lines from the play are quoted]

'The Confidential Clerk', *New York Herald Tribune*, (7 Feb 1954), section iv, 1 [T. S. Eliot's answers to questions concerning the play]

'T. S. Eliot on Life and its Paradoxes', *New York Times Magazine*, (21 Feb 1954), 16 [150 lines from *The Confidential Clerk*]

'The Confidential Clerk', *This Week*, (21 Feb 1954), 20 [Lines from the play are quoted, as captions to photographs of scenes from the play]

'The Three Voices of Poetry', *Atlantic*, cxciii/4 (April 1954), 38 [A condensed reprint of *The Three Voices of Poetry*, 1953]

'Clemenza per Ezra Pound: Una lettera di T. S. Eliot', *Il Mare*, xxxvi/1738 (31 Oct 1954), 1 [A letter about Ezra Pound, dated 14 Aug 1954]

'Books of the Year Chosen by Eminent Contemporaries', *Times*, (26 Dec 1954), 6

'*The Women of Trachis* by Ezra Pound: A Symposium', *Pound Newsletter*, 5 (Jan 1955), 3 [A contribution from T. S. Eliot]

'A Note on "In Parenthesis" and "The Anathemata" by David Jones', *Dock Leaves*, vi/16 (Spring 1955), 21 [A broadcast on Welsh Home Service of BBC, 29 October 1954]

'Le salut de trois grands poètes: Londres: T. S. Eliot', *Le Figaro Littéraire*, x/463 (5 March 1955), 1 [A tribute to Paul Claudel]

'The Literature of Politics', *Time and Tide*, xxxvi/17 (23 April 1955), 523 [Extracts from a speech made at a literary luncheon organized by the Education Advisory Committee of the London Conservative Union, 19 April 1955; Pubd 1955]

'Mr Donald Brace', *Times*, (27 Sept 1955), 11 [An obituary letter]

Letter, *Pound Newsletter*, 8 (Oct 1955), 7 [In homage to Ezra Pound on his 70th birthday]

'Fr. Cheetham Retires from Gloucester Road', *Church Times*, cxxxix/4856 (9 March 1956), 12 [Reprinted in rev. form as an obituary notice in *S. Stephen's Magazine*, May 1959]

'Eliot Text: "Expand Frontiers of Criticism"', *Minneapolis Morning Tribune*, lxxxix/343 (1 May 1956), 11 [The Gideon Seymour Memorial Lecture delivered at the University of Minnesota, 30 April 1956; pubd as *The Frontiers of Criticism*, 1956]

'Kipling and the O. M.', *Manchester Guardian*, (11 July 1956), 9

'Pygmalion', *Times*, (11 Dec 1956), 11

'The Importance of Wyndham Lewis', *Sunday Times*, (10 March 1957), 10

'Speech to the BBC Governors', *London Magazine*, iv/9 (Sept 1957), 54

'T. S. Eliot Gives a Unique Photo-Interview . . . Stepping Out a Little? I Like the Idea', *Daily Express*, (20 Sept 1957), 6 [On his method of work]

'Address at the Opening of the New University Library', *The University of Sheffield Fifty-fourth Annual Report to the Court*, (1958/59), 160

'T. S. Eliot Talks about His Poetry', *Columbia University Forum*, ii/1 (Fall 1958), 11 [Comments made in course of a reading of poetry by T. S. Eliot, 28 April 1958]

'Bishop Bell', *Times*, (14 Oct 1958), 13 [On Dr. Bell's proposal that T. S. Eliot should write a play (*Murder in the Cathedral*) for the Canterbury Festival; A postscript to Dr. Bell's obituary notice]

'Independent Television', *Times*, (11 Nov 1958), 11

'The Art of Poetry, I: T. S. Eliot', *Paris Review*, 21 (Spring/Summer 1959), 47

'The Unfading Genius of Rudyard Kipling', *Kipling Journal*, xxvi/129 (March 1959), 9 [An address delivered at annual luncheon of Kipling Society, 21 October 1958]

'Address', *From Mary to You*, (Dec 1959), 133 [An address delivered at the Centennial celebration of the Mary Institute in St. Louis, 11 Nov 1959]

'Una lettera di Eliot e la traduzione del titolo', *Sipario*, xiv/164 (Dec 1959), 76 [A letter, dated 9 July 1959, concerning the translation of the title, *The Elder Statesman*]

'The Influence of Landscape upon the Poet', *Daedalus*, lxxxix/2 (Spring 1960), 460 [Remarks made on receipt of the Emerson-Thoreau Award]

'Mr. Eliot's Progress', *Times Literary Supplement*, 3045 (8 July 1960), 433

'Mr. T. S. Eliot', *Sunday Express*, (31 July 1960), 4 [Denying the assertion that T. S. Eliot had changed his manner of living since his marriage to Valerie Fletcher, never seeing his former friends]

'Wyndham Lewis', *Observer*, (18 Dec 1960)

'Bruce Lyttleton Richmond', *Times Literary Supplement*, 3072 (13 Jan 1961), 17 [A tribute on the occasion of Richmond's 90th birthday]

'Sir Geoffrey Faber: A Poet among Publishers', *Times*, 1 April 1961), 12 [An obituary notice; Unsigned]

'New English Bible', *Times Literary Supplement*, 3087 (28 April 1961), 263

'New English Bible', *Times Literary Supplement*, 3089 (12 May 1961), 293

'New English Bible', *Times Literary Supplement*, 3091 (26 May 1961), 325

'New English Bible', *Times Literary Supplement*, 3094 (16 June 1961), 373

'Chatterly Prosecution a Blunder', *Times*, (3 July 1961), 6 [A report of the lecture, 'To Criticize the Critic' at Leeds, 1 July 1961, Quotes three paragraphs]

'Mögen Sie Picasso?', *Frankfurter allgemeine zeitung*, 245 (21 Oct 1961), supplement, 1 [T. S. Eliot's contribution to a symposium in honour of Picasso's 80th birthday]

'Miss Harriet Weaver', *Encounter*, xviii/1 (Jan 1962), 101 [An obituary tribute]

'New English Bible', *Times*, (24 March 1962), 9

'For Divine Reading', *Times*, (21 Aug 1962), 9 [On the New English Bible]

'Shakespeare's Tomb', *Times*, (4 Sept 1962), 11

'Shakespeare's Tomb', *Times*, (14 Sept 1962), 11

'Miss Sylvia Beach', *Times*, (13 Oct 1962), 10 [An obituary tribute; Reprinted in *Sylvia Beach, 1887–1962*, 1963]

Works List

' "Going into Europe": A Symposium', *Encounter*, xix/6 (Dec 1962), 65 [On Britain's entry into the Common Market]
'T. S. Eliot on the Language of the New English Bible: "Vulgar, Trivial, Pendantic . . . " ', *Sunday Telegraph*, 98 (16 Dec 1962), 7
'The "Cambridge School" and the New Morality', *Church Times*, cxlvi/5237 (28 June 1963), 12
'Mr Louis MacNeice', *Times*, (5 Sept 1963), 14 [An obituary notice]
'Edwin Muir: 1887–1959, An Appreciation . . . ', *Listener*, lxxi/1835 (28 May 1964), 872 [Reprinted as 'Preface' to *Selected Poems* by Edwin Muir, 1965]
'Letter to the Editor: A Memoir of T. S. Eliot', *New York Times Book Review*, (31 Jan 1965), 35 [An article by William Turney Levy; Includes quotations from letters]
'The Other T. S. Eliot', *Atlantic*, ccxv/5 (May 1965), 60 [article by Lawrence Durrell; includes quotations from letters]
'T. S. Eliot, 1888–1965', *Sewanee Review*, lxxiv/1 (Winter 1965/66 [A memorial issue; Contains reprint of *American Literature and the American Language*, 1953; Includes quotations from letters; Rev. and pubd as *T. S. Eliot: The Man and His Work*, 1966]
Ezra Pound: Selected Poems (Faber & Gwyer Ltd: London, 1928)
A Choice of Kipling's Verse (Faber & Faber Ltd: London, 1941) [Introduction reprinted in *On Poetry and Poets*, 1957]
Introducing James Joyce (Faber & Faber Ltd: London, 1942)
Literary Essays of Ezra Pound (Faber & Faber Ltd: London, 1954)
The Criterion, 1922–1939 (Faber & Faber Ltd: London, 1967)
'The Class Ode', *Harvard Class Day, 1910* (Cambridge, Massachusetts: Harvard University, 1910)
'The Love Song of J. Alfred Prufrock'; 'Portrait of a Lady'; 'The Boston Evening Transcript'; 'Hysteria'; 'Aunt Helen', *Catholic Anthology, 1914–1915*, ed. Ezra Pound (London: Elkin Mathews, 1915)
Introduction, *Le serpent*, Paul Valéry (London: R. Cobden-Sanderson, 1924)
Introduction, *Savonarola*, Charlotte Eliot (London: R. Cobden-Sanderson, 1926)
Introduction, *Seneca: His Tenne Tragedies*, ed. Charles Whibley (New York: Constable and Co. Ltd, 1927) [Reprinted in *Selected Essays, 1917–1932*, 1932]
Preface, *Of Dramatick Poesie*, John Dryden (London: Frederick Etchells & Hugh Macdonald, 1928)
Preface, *Fishermen of the Banks*, James B. Connolly (London: Faber & Gwyer, Ltd, 1928)
Preface, *This Americal World*, Edgar Ansel Mowrer (London: Faber & Gwyer Ltd, 1928)
Introduction, *The Wheel of Fire*, G. Wilson Knight (London: Oxford University Press, 1930)
Introduction, *Intimate Journals*, Charles Baudelaire (New York: Random House, 1930) [Reprinted as 'Baudelaire' in *Selected Essays 1917–1932*, 1932]

118

Introduction, *London: A Poem and the Vanity of Human Wishes*, Samuel Johnson (London: Frederick Etchells & Hugh Macdonald, 1930)

Introduction, *Pensées*, Blaise Pascal (New York: E. P. Dutton & Co. Inc., 1931) [Reprinted as 'The *Pensées* of Pascal' in *(Essays Ancient and Modern*, 1936]

'Donne in Our Time', *A Garland for John Donne*, ed. Theodore Spencer (Cambridge, Massachusetts: Harvard University Press, 1931)

Preface, *Bubu of Montparnasse*, Charles-Louis Philippe (Paris: Crosby Continental Editions, 1932)

Introduction, *Selected Poems*, Marianne Moore (New York: The Macmillan Company, 1935)

Introduction, *Poems of Tennyson* (London: Thomas Nelson and Sons Ltd, 1936) [Reprinted as 'In Memoriam' in *Essays Ancient and Modern*, 1936]

'A Note on the Verse of John Milton', *Essays and Studies by Members of the English Association, Vol. XXI*, ed Herbert Read (Oxford: The Clarendon Press, 1936) [Reprinted as 'Milton I' in *On Poetry and Poets*, 1957]

'Byron, 1788–1824', *From Anne to Victoria*, ed. Bonamy Dobrée (London: Cassell and Co. Ltd, 1937) [Reprinted as 'Byron' in *On Poetry and Poets*, 1957]

Introduction, *Nightwood*, Djuna Barnes (New York: Harcourt, Brace and Company, 1937)

'The Marching Song of the Pollicle Dogs'; 'Billy M'Caw: The Remarkable Parrot', *The Queen's Book of the Red Cross* (London: Hodder and Stoughton, 1939)

'XIII by T. S. Eliot', *Irving Babbitt, Man and Teacher*, eds Frederick Manchester and Odell Shepard (New York: G. P. Putnam's Sons, 1941)

'Towards a Christian Britain', *The Church Looks Ahead* ed. E. L. Mascall (London: Faber & Faber Ltd, 1941)

'To the Indians Who Died in Africa', *Queen Mary's Book for India* (London: George G. Harrap & Co. Ltd, 1943)

'Civilization: The Nature of Cultural Relation', *Friendship, Progress, Civilization* (London: The Anglo-Swedish Society, 1943) [An address delivered at the Anglo-Swedish Society luncheon, 18 March 1943]

'Cultural Forces in the Human Order', *Prospect for Christendom*, ed. Maurice B. Reckitt (London: Faber & Faber Ltd, 1945) [Rev. and reprinted as Chapter 1 of *Notes toward the Definition of Culture*, 1948]

'To Walter de la Mare', *Tribute to Walter de la Mare* (London: Faber & Faber Ltd, 1948)

Introduction, *All Hallow's Eve*, Charles Williams (New York: Pellegrini & Cudahy, 1948)

Preface, *James Joyce*, Bernard Gheerbrant (Paris: Lattune 1949)

Introduction, *The Adventures of Huckleberry Finn*, Samuel L. Clemens

(London: The Cresset Press, 1950)

'Ezra Pound'; 'Postscript, 1950', *Ezra Pound*, ed. Peter Russell (London: Peter Nevill Ltd, 1950)

Preface, *Murder in the Cathedral: A Screenplay* (London: Film Traders Ltd, 1951)

Introduction, *Leisure, The Basis of Culture*, Josef Pieper (London: Faber & Faber Ltd, 1952)

Preface, *The Need for Roots*, Simone Weil (London: Routledge & Kegan Paul Ltd, 1952)

'Literature Talk', *The Unity of European Culture* (London: BBC, 1953)

Foreword, *Contemporary French Poetry*, Joseph Chiari (Manchester: Manchester University Press, 1952)

Foreword, *Shakespeare*, Henri Fluchère (London: Longmans, Green and Co., 1953)

't. s. eliot'; 'pound books in print', *Ezra Pound at Seventy* (Norfolk, Connecticut: New Directions, 1956)

Introduction, *The Art of Poetry*, Paul Valéry (London: Pantheon Books, 1958)

Foreword, *Katherine Mansfield and Other Literary Studies*, J. Middleton Murry (London: Constable, 1959)

Foreword, *One-Way Song*, Wyndham Lewis (London: Methuen, 1960)

Preface, *A Selection of his Poems*, John Davidson (London: Hutchinson, 1961)

Introduction, *In Parenthesis . . .* , David Jones (London: Faber & Faber Ltd, 1961)

'Miss Sylvia Beach', *Sylvia Beach, 1887–1962*, eds Jackson Mathews and Maurice Seillet (Paris: Mecure de France, 1963)

'Tribute', *Aldous Huxley, 1894–1963*, ed. Julian Huxley (London: Chatto & Windus, 1965)

Bibliography

Aiken, C. *Ushant* (New York, 1952)

Aldington, R. *Life for Life's Sake: A Book of Reminiscences* (New York, 1941)
Stepping Heavenward (London, 1931)

Bell, Q. *Virginia Woolf, A Biography* (London, 1972)

Bergonzi, B. (ed.) *The Four Quartets: A Casebook* (London, 1969)
T. S. Eliot [Masters of World Literature series] (London, 1972)

Braybrooke, N. (ed.) *T. S. Eliot: A Symposium for his Seventieth Birthday* (London, 1958)

Browne Martin, E. *The Making of T. S. Eliot's Plays* (Cambridge, 1969)

Carswell, J. *Lives and Letters* (London, 1978)

Cox, C. B. and Hinchliffe, A. (eds) *The Waste Land: A Casebook* (London, 1971)

Crick, B. *George Orwell, A Life* (London, 1980)

Duncan, R. *How to Make Enemies* (London, 1968)

Eliot, V. (ed.) *T. S. Eliot: The Waste Land, a facsimile and transcript* (London, 1971)

Flower, N. (ed.) *Journals of Arnold Bennett* (London, 1932)

Forster, E. M. *Abinger Harvest* (London, 1936)

Gallup, D. *T. S. Eliot: a Bibliography* (London, 1969)

Gathorne-Hardy, R. (ed.) *Ottoline* (London, 1963)

Gilbert, S. (ed.) *Letters of James Joyce* (London, 1957)

Gordon, L. *Eliot's Early Years* (Oxford, 1977)

Guenther, J. *Sidney Keyes: a biographical enquiry* (London, 1967)

Hall, D. *Remembering Poets: reminiscences and opinions* (New York, 1978)

Hewison, R. *Under Siege, Literary Life in London 1939–45* (London, 1977)

Holroyd, M. *Lytton Strachey: a critical biography* (London, 1967)

Howarth, H. *Notes on some figures behind T. S. Eliot* (London, 1965)

Killorin, J. (ed.) *Selected Letters of Conrad Aiken* (Yale, 1978)

Leavis, F. R. *Anna Karenina and Other Essays* (London, 1967)

Levy Turner, W. and Scherle, V. *Affectionately, T. S. Eliot* (London, 1968)

Lewis Wyndham, P. *Blasting and Bombardiering* (London, 1937)

Marsh R. and Tambimuttu (compilers) *T. S. Eliot* (London, 1948)

Marx, G. *The Groucho Letters* (London, 1967)

Nicolson, N. (ed.) *Diaries and Letters of the Hon. Sir Harold Nicolson* (London, 1966–8)

Orwell, S. and Angus, I. (eds) *Collected Essays, Journalism and Letters of George Orwell* (London, 1968)

Paige, D. D. (ed.) *Selected Letters of Ezra Pound 1907–41* (London, 1951)

Plimpton, G. (ed.) *Writers and Their Work: The Paris Review interviews* (second series) (New York and London, 1963)

Rose, W. K. (ed.) *Letters of Wyndham Lewis* (London, 1963)

Russell, B. A. W. *Autobiography* (London, 1967)

Sencourt, R. *T. S. Eliot: A Memoir* (London, 1971)

Bibliography

Smidt, K. *Poetry and Belief in the Work of T. S. Eliot* (Oslo, 1949)

Smith, G. (ed.) *Letters of Aldous Huxley*, London, 1969)

Southam, B. C. (ed.) *Prufrock, Gerontion, Ash Wednesday and Other Poems: A Casebook* (London, 1978)

Spender, S. *The Thirties and After* (London, 1978)

　　　　T. S. Eliot [Penguin modern masters series] (London, 1976)

Stock, N. *The Life of Ezra Pound* (London, 1970)

Tate, A. (ed.) *T. S. Eliot, The Man and his Work* (London, 1967)

Vinson, J. (ed.) *Great Writers of the English Language* (London, 1979)

Woolf, L. *Beginning Again: An Autobiography of the Years 1911–1918* (London, 1964)

　　　　Downhill all the Way: An Autobiography of the Years 1919–1939 (London, 1967)

　　　　(ed.) *A Writer's Diary, being extracts from the Diary of Virginia Woolf* (London, 1953)

Acknowledgements

The author and publishers wish to thank the following who have kindly given permission for the use of copyright material:

The Estate of Conrad Aiken for extracts from *Ushant: An Essay*, and *Selected Letters*, ed. J. Killorin.

Faber and Faber Ltd and Mrs Valerie Eliot for extracts from various uncollected prose pieces and uncollected letters of T. S. Eliot. Copyright (c) Valerie Eliot 1983.

Faber and Faber Ltd for extracts from *After Strange Gods, Selected Essays, For Lancelot Andrewes: Essays on Style and Order, Thoughts After Lambeth* and *Essays Ancient and Modern* by T. S. Eliot.

Faber and Faber Ltd and Farrar, Straus & Giroux Inc. for extracts from *Knowledge and Experience in the Philosophy of F. H. Bradley, On Poetry and Poets*, and *To Criticise the Critic* by T. S. Eliot.

Faber and Faber Ltd and Harcourt Brace Jovanovich Inc. for extracts from *The Idea of a Christian Society, Notes Towards the Definition of Culture*, and *Selected Essays* by T. S. Eliot.

Faber and Faber Ltd and Harvard University Press for an extract from *The Use of Poetry and the Use of Criticism* by T. S. Eliot.

Faber and Faber Ltd and New Directions Publishing Corporation for extracts from *Selected Letters of Ezra Pound 1907–1941*, ed. D. D. Paige, Copyright 1950 by Ezra Pound.

Faber and Faber Ltd on behalf of the Ezra Pound Literary Property Trust and with New Directions Publishing Corporation for extracts from the journals *The Egoist*, iv, 5, and *The Criterion*, xi, 45.

Methuen & Co. Ltd for extracts from *The Sacred Wood* by T. S. Eliot.

Times Newspapers Ltd for the Obituary of T. S. Eliot published in *The Times* 5 Jan 1965.